Past Lives? This

Answering
the questions
mediums are
asked most

Spirit Medium
Michael G. Reccia

Happy Medium Press
www.happy-medium.co.uk

For Emma and Rebecca

*I look forward with excitement
to the great things you will both accomplish.*

Contents

7

It was a dark and not particularly stormy night...
An Introduction.

In fact, it wasn't stormy at all, but I've grabbed your attention, haven't I? Introductions to books are, in my experience, rarely trawled through but as a background to this volume the following few pages are, in my humble opinion, worthwhile reading. I do therefore hope you will take this introduction on board *first* rather than ploughing directly into the fast lane of this book.

The stormy bit is a complete fabrication but night it definitely was. I awoke (or so I thought) in the middle of this particular sleep period to find the bedroom ablaze with white light. I sat up in bed and nervously turned towards the door, watching in horror as it slowly opened of its own accord. My grandfather, dressed in his striped pajamas, drifted through it like a weightless feather, his body hovering in slow motion about twelve inches above the carpet. I could clearly see the gap between his bare feet and the floor. George (that's where the middle G. of my name comes from) floated across the curtained window, then turned, outstretched his arm and began to move towards me. At that point I cried out and everything suddenly went black. I awoke (again!) to discover my grandfather sitting up next to me in the big double bed I was sharing with him with a most concerned expression on his face. I was quite young at the time, perhaps only nine or ten years old, and was being looked after by my grandparents whilst my mother was away. I didn't realise it then but I had just watched my grandfather astral travelling. In other words, his spirit – the real *him* - had been out during the night whilst his physical body slept and my spiritual senses were acute enough to witness its return to his physical form.

I'd had a strange and disturbing childhood and occurrences like the one I've just described were not uncommon. For example, as a youngster I awoke one morning to see a huge 'someone' sitting in my bedside chair, the figure fading slowly away until all I was looking at was a pile of clothes. We moved house when I was fifteen, and in my bedroom at the new home I would regularly wake up in the early mornings to see a date – September 15 – scribbled in large, hand written letters across one of my bedroom walls. I would sit bolt upright, the sweat dripping down my face, and stare in horror as the spectral longhand gradually dissolved into nothingness. I *knew*, ahead of schedule, when things were going to happen, too. At night I would dream of little, seemingly inconsequential events - such as exactly what combination of letters and parcels would be arriving in the morning post for me; and also of more significant happenings, such as the unannounced arrival, the day after I had dreamt of it, of my aunt and uncle on our doorstep, when I genuinely believed them to still be overseas and hadn't seen them for years (my uncle was a warrant officer with the RAF and he and my aunt travelled the world). The 'special' dreams I had always proved to be correct.

Until my early twenties I was achingly shy, petrified of crowds (it was as though the sheer weight of all those random thoughts leaking out from so many chaotic minds completely overwhelmed me), and I blushed whenever anyone spoke to me. I knew that I was, at the very least, psychic (although I didn't fully understand what that term meant) and suspected I was also quite, quite mad. It was not until my late twenties, at a time when my marriage was falling apart and I sought sanity, sanctuary and distance from the situation for a few days at my aunt and uncle's house on the coast* that I realised I wasn't mad at all. There was a name for my condition, explained my aunt, and the name was *medium*. During my stay my aunt and uncle calmly announced one day that that evening they would be attending a service at the local spiritualist church. Did I want to go with them? At first I emphatically told them that I didn't. I had been brought up as a strict catholic and imagined a spiritualist meeting to be some spooky event at which people sat in the dark and things flew around the room. However, such was the state of my nerves and physical health at that time that I was not in a fit condition to stay in the house by myself. I craved company – *any* company - and I therefore reluctantly agreed to accompany my relatives on that fateful night.

To cut a long story short the medium taking the service that evening, working in a friendly, brightly lit, loving atmosphere punctuated by elderly ladies bearing cups of tea, came to me from the platform and told me that, within five years, *I* would be doing what she was doing. "You will transform," she said. "You will transfigure. And you will become a medium many other mediums will look up to."

Somehow I knew she had given me accurate information. I was simultaneously thrilled and frightened by it. After my divorce came through I determined to learn more about the special gift I had been given. I began to attend a church circle (a regular gathering of like-minded people who sit in a circle supervised by a medium in order to communicate with the spirit worlds and/or to develop their spiritual gifts). The weekly event was overseen by a crusty, middle aged man who became a close friend (Bruce has now, sadly for me, passed to the higher side of life). During one meeting I met with a lady, a newcomer who I instantly recognised, although I knew I had never seen her before in this life. We chatted and she invited me home to meet her husband, the three of us subsequently becoming firm friends and myself a frequent visitor to their house. She then took me into her front room and explained that she had been sitting (as in sitting with the intent of developing her spiritual gifts) in that room regularly by herself for over thirty years, during which time she had taught herself to meditate and to communicate with the spirit people she had been seeing since she was a girl. "If you wish to develop for the right reasons," she said. "If you want to help people, then I will sit with you once a week and teach you everything I have discovered. It will take discipline and dedication and commitment. What do you say?"

I said *yes*, and then sat with Joan in that room – a room that was alive with spiritual power – every Sunday, come rain or shine, for a full seven years from the time of her initial invitation. During those years I was shown how to meditate, how to interpret the information that came to me *clairvoyantly* (through spirit sight), *clairaudiently* (through spirit hearing) and *clairsentiently* (through spirit sensing). I was also taught to understand myself and my physical mind and to control my mind and the energies and impressions and insights that, up to that point in my life, had controlled me. I was then invited to take my first service at a local spiritualist church. Standing there after the service in front of a church congregation comprised of strangers, friends and family – something I could never have done seven years earlier - I knew that I had found my purpose in life and that all that had gone before had been a preparation for this moment and many more like it. I knew that the path I was now on would never let me go, nor did I wish it to.

A comparatively short time after that first service i left my high-paid, high powered employment as a director of a large advertising agency to become a full time medium. At the time of writing this introduction I have served God[§] for some twenty years, around twelve of those on a full time basis. My service for Higher Authority has consisted of church work, giving private and postal readings, clearing disturbed houses, teaching meditation, giving lectures, holding workshops and seminars, producing CDs on a variety of spiritual topics and, at times, working as part of a team during the night in order to release into the light spirits who are 'stuck' or do not realise they are 'dead'. The teaching aspect of my mediumship is extremely important to me. I have an inquiring mind and, having discovered all those years ago that I was not mad but mediumistic, I decided not only to develop my gift but also to investigate it, to become fully conversant with its workings, to probe the reasons for me having been given it and to unearth and understand the deeper implications behind spirit communication. Both hell and high water have been traversed in order to bring me the understanding of things I was seeking. Being a medium is not easy. Being a medium who constantly seeks to understand *more* about his craft and about the nature of – well – *everything* is even more difficult. We learn through experience and – *boy* – have I gone through some experiences in my pursuit of spiritual knowledge!

Part of my work today involves conducting 'question and answer' sessions at spiritualist churches and other venues where people who are seeking a greater understanding of spirit communication, of the mechanics and realities of life behind and beyond this physical existence, of the natural spiritual laws we operate within and – at our peril – go against at times, and who wish to ponder and find answers to the age-old questions *who am I*; *what am I*; *why am I here*; *where am I going* and *what can I do to make things better here, both for myself and for others*, can, with the help of the guiding spirits who inspire me and give me the benefit of their wisdom on such occasions, add to their spiritual knowledge.

Those Q & A sessions are so popular, with so many of the questions from the audiences cropping up again and again at so many different venues that, for me, they confirm my conviction that we as mediums ought to be working hard not just to provide evidence of life after death, but also to add a new quality to *this* life by seeking to explain how we do what we do and answering some of those perennial questions that hover on the lips of so many souls who desire greater spiritual understanding and inner peace. Hence my decision to publish as my first book a volume that is not about my life as a medium (why on earth would you wish to read about *my* life and about *me*? Writing such a book might massage *my* ego but how would it benefit *you?*[†]) but concerns the things I have discovered during my spiritual journey (and believe with all my be-ing[¶] – all my inner *knowing* – to be true) regarding existence, the nature of consciousness and the way things work spiritually, not just for mediums, but for us all. Each of the answers to the questions featured in this book offers information that has, as its source, prayer for guidance and inspiration, the input of my spirit guides and/or the angels who sometimes work behind the scenes with me and very occasionally take my breath away by revealing their presence, or of other teachers from the realms of light who, on occasion, use me as a conduit. If I have been uncertain in any way about any detail during the writing of this book I have asked and received, and have repeatedly questioned my words and refined the text until a sufficient amount of relevant information has been forthcoming regarding each topic.

Of course, one could write a complete book – or series of books – about each and every subject covered in these pages. However, the purpose of this volume is to provide succinct and informative answers to every question so that each topic makes sense to the reader without giving them a headache, is answered effectively, and allows space for more questions to be addressed and answered in the pages that follow! Also, at some stage the writing process must stop in order to allow the reading process to take place.

Any questions you might like answered in a companion volume can be sent to me via my website:
http://www.happy-medium.co.uk
or you can email me at:
michael@happy-medium.co.uk

I can't reply to any of yur questions personally, I'm afraid – creation is a demanding Boss – but you just might find them addressed in the next book.

Finally, thank you for choosing this one.

God Bless,
M. G. R.
January 2005

Yes, the same ones. On that day many years earlier when they had put in an unexpected appearance, my aunt had insisted I turn up on their doorstep unannounced should I ever be in trouble. She drummed this into me with the insistence of someone who, psychically, knew that one day I would need to take up that invitation.

§ *You'll find quite a few mentions of God in this book. Mediums* work with *and not* for *guides or angels. Nor do guides and angels work for mediums. We all work for the Big Guy as a team. He calls the shots.*

† *Oh, all right then. Maybe one day.*

¶ *You will notice the word being appears hyphenated – be-ing – in many instances throughout this book. This is not a typographical error but a reference to not only an individual, but also to that individual's continuous state of existing as a consciousness.*

Question: A person has been married twice during their life on earth. Or perhaps even three times. Which husband/wife will they be with when they pass over?

A. In order to answer this question we must first understand that the close earthly relationships we are used to and comfortable with – those of *husbands, wives, sons, daughters, grandparents*, etc. – are just that... *earthly* relationships. True, behind those relationships there lies a great spiritual bonding and love and purpose, and the special people around you on earth – family and friends, and even valued work colleagues – interact with you and are linked to you by *design*, not by accident, but we have to appreciate that these earthly 'name tags' are meaningless when applied to spiritual relationships once a certain level of higher consciousness has been reached. What does matter in spiritual relationships – what *always matters* – is the law of love. If love has truly existed between you and certain other people in your life, whether that love has brought you together through family relationships or through friendship links, then the mutual wish to continue to share in each other's existence that you currently experience on earth extends beyond this physical life. The love link, according to spiritual law, automatically allows people who truly love each other access to each other in the spirit realms. Even if you are on differing levels of be–ing, of evolution according to the progress of your individual souls, you will be able to meet with each other and enjoy each other's company under certain conditions which will regularly be made available to you.

Upon passing into the spirit worlds you will make new friends but will naturally also choose to spend time in the company of people who once were and are once again special to you, and you to them, and to be close to each other on the higher side of life, without living in each other's pockets. You may also decide to travel onwards together (i.e. to learn and to evolve together as souls) in 'family' units or groups comprising of yourself and certain of these 'significant others' from your life on earth. Freed from the confines of earthly relationships, where sexual jealousy frequently raises its ugly head, as often does the imposition of the will of one soul onto another, you will find in the spirit worlds that you sometimes form relationships and ties of love – i.e. mutually attractive harmonies of vibration – that you would not have considered viable or even morally acceptable whilst on earth. As an example, it is not unusual within the higher spheres of consciousness to see spirits who once lived on earth as – say – a husband and his two former wives now co–existing and moving onwards together in a state of complete joy. Or to come across souls who were formerly husband and wife on earth now sharing their spiritual existence not only with each other but also with a former admirer and rival for the affections of one of the two souls, and loving each other equally as a unit of three, if all three are sufficiently of one mind regarding where they want to go next (i.e. how they wish to evolve as souls and where they want their spiritual evolution to take them) and by what spiritual means they wish to get there.

The converse of this law of attraction also applies, in that *you do not have to be with anyone you do not want to be with* in the spirit realms, no matter how much the other party may wish to re-establish their earthly control over you or to reconnect to you. It takes two to make a love connection. Therefore, the husband who has been dominated and browbeaten by his wife during their earthly marriage, or the wife who has been physically abused by her spouse before death separated them and ended her suffering, need have no fear that their wedding certificate, or the confining dictates of a religion stating that their marriage is forever, will condemn them to an eternity of forced, renewed companionship and mutual loathing once the remaining partner passes to the spirit side of life. A marriage certificate is merely a piece of paper. A true marriage can exist only where love is present on both sides, and there are many different kinds of 'marriage' – of agreed and desired co-existence in the name of love – on the higher side of life.

I must stress that the above information regarding the shedding of earthly 'name tags' and the gradual growing away from earthly relationships as we understand them should not be a cause for concern to those people longing to meet their departed mothers, fathers, brothers, sisters, children and friends again once they leave this earth. If true love (which is *spiritual* love) existed between you and your loved ones they will be there for you and will appear to you just as you remembered them at their best. It is simply a matter of recognising that, in the larger scale of things, 'mother', 'father', 'brother', 'sister', etc., are earthly terms only, convenient 'labels' those people wore whilst you were connected to them on earth *for a purpose*. You will see them as you used to see them and regard them for a time as being in exactly the same relationship with you as they were whilst you were both in this life, but you will also eventually see them (and yourself) as the spirits – the beings of light – you really are, the beautiful end products of many existences and many relationships. You will discover that the love links between you and those you cared about whilst on earth are deeper, more permanent and more wondrous and joyful than could ever be expressed or experienced within the confines of a single physical life. Your spiritual family will always be linked to you in love, will always be there for you and you can never lose them or be truly separated from them.

So – who will the twice or thrice-married husband or wife be with upon passing from this earth? Perhaps with both former partners. Perhaps with all three. Perhaps with none of them. It's a matter of choice for all concerned and – above all – a matter of true love.

Question: Do you believe in soul mates?

A. I'm often asked this question with the focus on some new potential love interest who has recently entered the life of the person I am 'sitting' with (i.e. conducting a reading for) and with the sitter either having been told that this new someone is their 'soul mate' by some dubious spiritual 'expert', or them feeling a special and exciting empathy towards the person, invariably in a romantic sense, which they attribute to some irresistible spiritual attraction. Sometimes sitters ask me if they will *ever* meet their soul mate – longing constantly for that perfect romantic liaison that has its roots in infinity and will guarantee them a relationship on earth that will last a lifetime then continue on forever in harmony and happiness in the worlds beyond.

I try to be as gentle as possible when explaining that, in my experience, the starry-eyed concept of a 'soul mate', i.e. someone you will inevitably meet on earth who can be regarded as the other half of you and is your perfect partner, in the romantic or sexual sense, now and forever, simply does not – *cannot* – exist. Does this mean that you will never find love or a compatible partner? Of course not. Does this mean you will never meet up again with souls who you have already known and loved in some past existence? Not at all. It should be understood, however, that if you are destined to meet and to be with someone in this life in a one-to-one relationship it is *always* in order that you and that person might learn from each other whilst here on earth. If mutually desired spiritual growth between two souls can be best served by them coming together in a husband and wife or love-partnership situation during their earthly incarnations, then your 'accidental' meeting with the person with whom you are to form such a relationship will inevitably draw you into that predetermined partnership so that within it major soul lessons may be learned through your shared experiences.

In considering the question of soul mates we must remember that we are *all*, in fact, part of the same thing – we are each an individualisation of God consciousness and creativity, emanating from the same One source, so in a very real sense we are *all* soul mates. We are all linked to each other in a binding and unbreakable way that we rarely acknowledge or understand the truth of whilst on earth. We must remember, too, that as we as souls experience and work through various levels of existence and consciousness, we gravitate increasingly towards other souls who are just like us in outlook and purpose, coming together to eventually form 'group souls' in order that we might delight in each other's company and learn valuable lessons within a group for the purpose of the linked spiritual progression of that whole loving soul 'family'. (*Also see entry on Group Souls, page 67.*)

Often several members of a group soul will incarnate at around the same time, although not always in the same area of the world and not always with the intention of meeting up during their lives on earth. These incarnated group members come here to learn lessons collectively for the benefit and progression of the whole group and, on occasion, *do* meet and recognise – *remember* – each other. That recognition usually manifests itself not as feelings of romantic love, however, but as a knowing within that *here is a person I have shared an existence with before somewhere*, a person I am comfortable with, a person I am in harmony with. For example, I have, during this lifetime, met one person from my group soul to whom I was married in a previous life (I have a vivid memory of our collective demise, as does she. I can tell you where we lived and can even describe the curtains and furnishings in the large house that was ours for a time.). In this incarnation that person is considerably older than myself, was instrumental in my development as a medium, and has never been looked upon in a romantic way by me or vice versa. She is, in effect, one of my 'group soul mates', with that term having nothing to do with the bonding of souls in a romantic sense on earth and everything to do with ongoing spiritual love. In other past existences (revealed to us by guides) she has been my brother and also my female associate in an ancient religious organisation. Do you see the distinction between this definition of a soul mate and the romantic definition most people associate with the term? People usually want to find a 'soul mate' because they are looking for the perfect romantic liaison, not realising that romantic love belongs to this plane of consciousness only. The 'group soul mate' who is a part of

24

my life at this moment has been my associate, my brother, my wife and my teacher, linking to me in both this existence and other physical lifetimes I have experienced. I do not think of her in any way romantically, yet her soul and mine are connected as a small part of a great organisation of souls travelling forwards into infinity together.

There are other people outside of blood ties I have met during my life's journey who have also become every bit as close to me as family members and represent relationships that I desire to go on forever and extend beyond this physical life. My feelings for these souls are so strong that I believe I have known them in existences other than this one and that we were supposed to meet during this life. Again, however, these relationships are not physical or romantic in any way and involve souls of both sexes. There are bound to be such people in your life, the type of love you feel for them having nothing to do with romantic fulfilment or sexual yearning or needing someone to end your loneliness and everything to do with an affinity that you instinctively feel stretches beyond the limits of this small existence.

There is a need for extreme caution here, particularly from those of you who are just setting out on the journey that will allow you to develop your spiritual gifts. I have seen people get into all kinds of tangles because they have been told that 'such and such' is their soul mate (in the romantic sense). I have also, many years ago, been the focus for mischief in this area from the other side *personally*, with messages supposedly from guides (and in actuality from devious and un-evolved entities on the lower astral plane, boosted by the manipulative wishes of people here on earth) telling me that a person I was sitting with at the time for spirit communication was my 'soul mate'. In the interests of shocking you sufficiently into super-cautiousness, I will let you in on a little secret. Some considerable time ago, as a young and inexperienced medium, I was almost sucked into a deliberate psychic trap – a manipulative, controlling situation that saw me come to within three weeks of actually *marrying* someone I did not love, simply because I had been told that we were supposed to be together – that we were *soul mates*. It's a long story, and one that, in the interests of keeping you on the right spiritual track, is told in greater depth elsewhere in this book. (*Also see entry on Spirit Possession, page 89.*)

My experience is not unique. I have frequently seen similar things happen to both mediums and initiates alike. Always – *always* – use your common sense in *any* relationship, from a friendship to an affair of the heart, and realise that no source from the spirit world acting on behalf of the light – no spiritually enlightened guide or angel or family member who has passed on – will ever tell you that this person is for you or that you are supposed to be with that person. It simply isn't done – so *beware*! Beware, too, of advertising in the media claiming that someone can find your 'soul mate' for you by talking clairvoyantly to your guides and to their guides and, acting on instruction from those matchmaking spiritual sources, then introduce you to the right person for you. Be taken in by such advertisements and I guarantee your wallet will soon be pounds lighter and that you will also be heading for deep and dangerous waters.

To sum up – 'soul mates' in the romantic sense? *Nope.* Soul mates as in souls you have known before this life, will know again in future existences and with whom you share a wonderful affinity, harmony and sense of purpose? *Definitely.*

Question: What are your

views on reincarnation?

A. Do I believe in reincarnation?

From the number of times I have been told about or shown aspects of past existences by a communicator from the spirit worlds whilst reading for someone I have to say, "*Yes, I do.*"

Sometimes, as was the case with one particular young lady, a significant scenario from a past life will play itself out before my eyes so that I can pass the details on to the sitter. In the lady's case, as I sat with her I was suddenly shown a vision of troubled waters by one of her guides. I could then quite clearly see a ship at sea in a storm. The vessel was listing and already halfway under the waves. Trying to be diplomatic, I asked the lady if she was afraid of drowning, as this was also being imparted to me clairsentiently.

"It's my worst nightmare," she replied. "I'm terrified of death by drowning."

I was then told by her guide that she frequently had bad dreams in which she felt she was drowning and she confirmed that this was correct.

"Well," I said, "there's no need whatsoever to fear death

by drowning this time around – it isn't going to happen – *you've already done it!*"

The guide, as I continued to talk to the young woman, made me aware of the fact that she had gone down with the ship during the incident that was being 'replayed' from a previous lifetime. He went on to tell me that she had been a man during that existence and that she (he!) had become trapped below decks and was unable to open the hatches and escape. He explained that she was claustrophobic in this lifetime and, again, she confirmed that this was very much the case. I reassured her, as a result of the guide's promptings, that her recurrent nightmares, fear of drowning and claustrophobia were simply 'echoes' from this previous existence and, by the end of the reading, she said she felt very relieved and far calmer as a result of the background knowledge that had been given to her by her guide.

Sometimes I am guided to a physical defect on a sitter's body that I have no knowledge of (such as a scar on the head under the hairline, or on the stomach, or a patch of skin of a different colour or a hidden birthmark somewhere on the sitter's person) and told that this is also a physical 'echo' of something that happened to that person in a former existence. In many cases an unexplained scar in this lifetime (one that cannot be attributed to any injury sustained at any time during the sitter's present incarnation) can indicate the area of a wound or injury sustained in a previous one. Similarly, discomfort or lack of feeling in a certain part of the body that can neither be cured nor diagnosed can be an indication of harm or injury having been caused to that area in a previous existence.

Further weight for the argument of reincarnation being a fact is also frequently added during readings when guiding influences who come through to communicate with a sitter explain that they have been linked to that person in a previous physical existence, the two of them having once lived on earth at the same time. Sometimes guide and sitter have previously been father and son, or two brothers or sisters, or pupil and teacher, or any number of other close-knit combinations, with the spirit communicator now choosing to help the person on earth as a guide. (*Also see entry on Group Souls, page 67.*)

I also find it difficult to argue against reincarnation when I have distinct memories from two very different lifetimes *myself...* and *no*, I'm afraid I wasn't Henry the VIII or Cleopatra! That so many people seem to have been rulers and famous people in their past existences (often the same ones!) is a constant source of amusement to me. With regard to past life regression we must remember that we are all psychic, whether we acknowledge the fact or not, and that certain of us are also mediumistic, without necessarily having a conscious knowledge of that fact at a time when we choose to undergo a 'past life regression'. The mediumistic mechanism still operates without our conscious choice. We are spirits and we sense and interpret things with our spiritual senses on a higher vibration, translating them down to our physical ones. Therefore, in certain cases of 'regression', I believe the person is picking up not on the circumstances of a past life that *they* have experienced, but on impressions transmitted by another spirit in a clairvoyant manner, or on information that remains 'embedded' in the atmosphere, much as an old fashioned tape head picks up impressions from the magnetic tape it comes into contact with.

In two of *my* past lives (I have memories of two and details of a third, courtesy of my guides) I was quite an ordinary soul (though considerably more wealthy in one of them than I am now!) and a member of a privileged order – which had nothing to do with fame – in the third, which is the furthest one back according to how we measure time.

Now, having said that I believe in reincarnation, I should make it clear that I do not hold with the belief of many people and religions that reincarnation means endless death *from* and rebirth *to* this level of consciousness, one life seamlessly following another, until we 'get it right' and earn the right to move onwards and upwards. Everything we do which affects our soul, in my experience of spiritual 'mechanics', is a matter of choice and of free will, so it is my strong opinion, as a logical extrapolation of God's universal law of free will, that we only come back here to earth if we have first agreed to do so, and then not to partake in an end-to-end cycle of countless lives. We are never forced to do *anything* we don't wish to do once we leave this planet and I also believe there are many alternatives to an earthly incarnation – other 'routes' we can choose – that give us equal opportunities to evolve as souls without having to repeatedly experience this plane in a physical body. These alternatives are, again, a matter of our choice, with our decisions regarding them being taken in our own time.

Finally, there is a tendency in some circles today to place far too much importance on who we *were*. Yes, in the case of the young lady mentioned earlier and others like her, the past life information was liberating and helped her to feel more at peace and to better understand herself in *this* incarnation. We have to remember, however, that an incarnation is rather like a suit of clothes that is worn for a special occasion. We are the *wearer*, not the suit of clothes. By all means investigate your past lives if you feel the need to. Be curious. Seek the answers but be aware that those past lives have served their purpose. From them you have gained whatever experiences you were supposed to gain and you have moved on – grown out of them – leaving those simple suits of clothes behind.

The point of power – the moment at which you can make a difference to yourself and to others and to this world – is *now*. It is your present life and your present and future challenges that are of vital importance to the future of your soul and you have to be careful not to waste it or them by living in the past.

Question: What happens to children who have passed over to the spirit world before reaching adulthood? Often it is said that they 'grow up' on the spirit side of life. If they are spirits, why should they need to 'grow up'?

A. The answer to this question lies in asking a further question regarding our essential nature as beings, and that is: What, exactly, *are* we? We are spirits, of course, and not the flesh and blood we appear to be – but just what *is* a spirit? What is a spirit composed of? What are the building blocks, the materials, that make up a spirit? *What are you made of,* spiritually speaking, dear reader? At its most simplistic the answer is: 'you are a vibration'. But a vibration of *what,* exactly? You are an individual and unique resonance – an oscillation – of God energy, an expression of God light. You are motion against the stillness; recognising yourself through the ripples you make within the great, calm ocean of be-ing that is God consciousness. Your true, essential form (i.e. relating to your *essence*) as a spirit is not human in shape or appearance at all. We are made in God's image, yes, but whatever makes us think that God's image is a humanoid one? Isn't it more honest to say that it comforts us to think of

God as being a *be-ing* in *our* image, when in truth the ages old concept of an old man with a beard sitting on a throne, or any other human-looking representations, are very limited, biased interpretations that try to condense the reality of God into something we can relate to? The human form is just one *aspect* – one *projection* – of God–creation and manifestation, but your essence – your spiritual core, is, for want of a better expression, formless. An analogy to you as a spirit could be made to a sphere of light. Or to a field of pure energy and consciousness. Or to a unique frequency of *be-ing*. You as a spirit on earth are the indefinable and inseparable – a part of the infinite; of *God* – choosing to define itself temporarily through the illusion of individuality and separation – your physical and mental life here – in order to evolve. You are a spark of God consciousness born into the illusion of individuality and connected for a time to a flesh and blood body that is not really you. That spark of light, that unique vibration, is what is permeating and motivating your physical body and your physical mind at this moment. It is the real you.

When you 'die' from this world that real you migrates to a more rapid – a finer – vibration of 'reality', one that it has earned the right to harmonise with, one that does not have to rely on such dense matter as is manifest in the physical universe in order to express and recognise itself. You will still appear to have a human body and form whilst in your new surroundings (except when you choose to manifest yourself in other ways, by bringing into view other aspects of soul

34

expression, of course). That human form, however, as with your present human form, will simply be a projection of the real you. It is a suit of clothes, if you like, an image that you will bring forth from your soul memory subconsciously of a form you have grown familiar and comfortable with whilst on earth; a form that can easily be recognised and related to by yourself and by those who have known you here and will prefer to interface with you through this familiar projection of the real you on the inductive levels of the higher side of life. However far you progress into eternity and infinity, the real – whole – you is always the essence behind the projections you will bring forth in order to relate to yourself, to other souls and to your surroundings, and never the limitation of the projections themselves.

I have often clairvoyantly and clairaudiently seen and heard children from the higher side of life. They frequently come through to sitters during readings and sometimes, having first established with the sitter the physical age they had reached at the point when they passed, and who they were, will then, in the blink of an eye, transform into an older version of the same person. Similarly, highly evolved guides can sometimes seem to the clairvoyant eye to be constantly shifting in age, identity, and even sex, morphing from young to old, male to female, from one ethnic set of characteristics to another, as they communicate. This is because the medium is reading and being presented with *aspects of who those spirits are and have been*; facets of their real form; projections from some of the lives they have lived on earth that remain as identifying echoes within their soul makeup. They wear the triumphs of their past lives (for it is the challenges of these lives, successfully encountered, that have enabled them to evolve into their present form) like brilliant jewels of light and colour emanating from their principal chakra points, and can choose, from their jewel box of achievement, which aspects of themselves they wish to project when contacting this earth through a medium.

We have to remember that, although we have been born and have reached a certain age on earth as human beings during our present incarnation, our physical bodies and minds are merely 'solidified' (to the human eye) and temporary projections – they are suits of clothes and *not who we really are*. As another analogy, most of you drive a car, but you are always the driver, never the car. The car is a vehicle, nothing more. Similarly, the human body is a vehicle which you steer and drive through physical life. You are in the driving seat but you are not the physical body or the physical mind. We have to remember, too, that our spirit has acquired an 'age' (measured not by time but by maturity of experience and rate of vibration) since it issued forth from God consciousness and an identity that is quite independent of our physical age, appearance and identity on earth. As you read this you may be a young soul in a physical body that has grown old. Or an ages–old soul in a still-young earthly body. You don't know who you really are and can seldom perceive on this level, unless you have developed your spiritual gifts, who the people around you really are from a spiritual standpoint.

Bearing all this is mind, the children we have known who have passed to spirit as children – as with every person we will ever link to on this level of consciousness – have only been relating to us on a physical level via a *single facet* of *who they really are as a soul* whilst they were a part of our lives on earth. Once they reach the appropriate level of consciousness on the spirit side of life; that point where their soul history and memories are once again accessible to them, they may choose to take on an appearance they had in a life that we, not having had access to their whole soul history, will be completely unaware of. Were they to come through to us clairvoyantly 'wearing' this appearance we would not recognise them, so they present themselves during a clairvoyant session first as the child they once were on earth so that we can relate to them, then, having established their identity, they may choose to show themselves to us at different ages, or even as different personalities, or to remain as that child whilst they communicate, dependent on our levels of understanding and acceptance.

Sometimes a soul will very quickly regain access to knowledge of the other facets of its soul identity upon passing over; sometimes the process takes a little longer as we understand the passage of time. A child may therefore happily linger, upon passing over, with those members of the earthly family it was incarnated into and who have also passed into spirit for a time before assuming its true soul identity and appearance, and may 'grow up' as it would have done on earth according to the concept of time and experience having passed as perceived by itself and by those family members who surround it. Remember that those family members will be progressing towards greater understanding of their true selves at different rates too. If they are still quite closely bound to a sense of time and change of appearance as dictated by an earthly time clock, the child dwelling in their midst will change its outward illusion of age according to their belief (i.e. their mental expectations and impressions will have an effect upon the child's self perception and therefore its outward form – its *projection*) of how old that child should be as their perception of time passes. In actual fact it is merely the outward projection of that spirit that appears to grow and change, not the actual spirit. Also, consider that any child who passes has *the mind of a child* at that point, just as you will take with you the mental understanding and perspective of a person of a certain age and experience when you pass over. To develop beyond that point a spirit has to be gently and slowly made aware of its greater aspects and its history as a be-ing; gently led out of the mind set it may find itself in at the point of passing to higher consciousness. Hence the need to mature in thought and realisation of changed circumstance – the need to 'grow up' in some respects – or perhaps a better description would be to 'grow away' from the earth and restrictions of the recent earth life in modes of thinking. Whilst this process of change is taking place the child will still regard itself as a child, as will many of the people around it. Once that spiritual maturity of thought has been restored to the child/spirit, however, it will take a leap forward in recognition of who it really is and will be reunited with – will rediscover – its soul memory. The length of time it takes for spirits who have passed over as children to *remember who they really are*, and therefore to be once more in touch with their greater selves, and the sum of all their experiences, varies from spirit to spirit.

Does this mean that bereaved parents will one day, upon leaving this world, be confronted by a child they no longer recognise – and that a long yearned for reunion will not, in fact, take place? Will they instead meet someone totally alien to them who insists that he or she is their long lost offspring? Not at all. The spirit of the child will appear to them in familiar guise for as long as it is deemed necessary by all parties concerned and thenceforth in a recognised form as its greater self. Our sons, daughters, mothers, fathers, grandfathers, grandmothers, brothers, sisters, etc., will appear to us exactly as they did on earth (though bodily whole, sound, and, in many cases, younger than we remember them, according to their inward preferences of how their outward projection should look) but will also one day be revealed to us in all their soul glory as will we to them. We will never lose those aspects of and contact with the close family members that we have cherished and loved. Rather, the spirits we love in family and friendship will be around us in far greater glory and radiate greater harmony with us than we could ever have imagined whilst relating to them on earth. The love link – the spiritual bond – is eternal.

Question: What is my guide's name? Why don't guides or, sometimes, family members and friends who are communicating from the spirit side of life through a medium, always give their names?

A. Think about your own given name for a moment or two. Quietly and carefully examine its written form, its sound and its significance as a part of your identity, in your imagination. You will have a first name, perhaps a middle name, and certainly a surname. Those names – those precise arrangements of letters (and phonetic sounds when spoken) – help you to identify yourself as an individual within earthly society and also link you through the written and spoken word to your earthly parents, your greater family and your family history – your lineage. In addition to friends and family all kinds of people, from employers to bankers, doctors to dentists, salesmen to solicitors, all refer to you by your name. Your name is a universally accessible focal point which, when spoken out loud or thought about or written down by those who know you well, instantly conjures up an image of you, with your unique face, body, voice, personality and mannerisms, in the minds of those who use it. Our names are very important to us here on earth. Besides being a reference and mental connection point for ourselves, our family and our colleagues, they are also used as an identification 'badge' that links us uniquely to things we regard as 'ours', from credit cards to driving licences to medical records, and to a thousand other aspects of earthly life we need a name in order to take advantage of.

In spirit 'society' things are slightly different. Consider the question of reincarnation. (*Also see entry on Reincarnation, page 28.*) If you have lived on earth a number of times (i.e. reincarnated) it must also follow that you will have been known by a number of different names – by one (at least!) during each of those separate lifetimes. In your current incarnation, for the sake of argument, you might be called Fred Smith. In a former life on earth, however, you might have been known as *Elizabeth Shaw*, or *Hans Mueller*, or *Runs In The Fields*. Which of those people is the real you? Which of those names is your one, true name? Well, actually *none* of them from a spiritual standpoint. The names that have been assigned to you at various stages during the evolution of your soul on earth by the people around you during those lives have been temporary labels attributed to the numerous manifestations of you that have appeared on the earth plane (that is not to play down the important role those names have played in the growth of your soul, however, as each of them, as with everything specifically attributed to you on earth, will have had an underlying spiritual significance at those times in your soul's development when you were known by them). You, however, are the soul *behind* those names, *behind* those personalities, each of which has been a projection into this physical world of your true, greater self. Upon leaving this world you may continue to use and feel comfortable with your present earthly name for a time, but as you grow in knowledge and rediscovery of your greater self, you will realise that that name only applies to one small facet of the be-ing you really are. As you continue to evolve, your current name will be something you will use only rarely – perhaps only when communicating with someone through a medium so that the sitter – your relative or friend who is still experiencing an earthly incarnation – may recognise you.

Many sitters, intrigued by the concept of having a guide, ask me if that guide will give them a name. I then explain that guides have reached a stage in their spiritual evolution, as will we all eventually, where they are known – *identified* – not by any earthly name at all, but rather by the unique light signature that emanates from their principal energy centres (chakras) and their auras. It is this 'fingerprint' of light, an expression of their past experience and evolution, by which they are recognised in the spirit realms. "Ah," you will say, "but my guide has given his or her name to me." – and I don't doubt that they have. Knowing the workings of earthly society and our ingrained, deep-seated need to link a name to each person we know so that we can identify them and paint a mental picture of them when we are not in their presence, a guide often *will* give sitters a name. In spiritual reality, however, any name given, whether or not it was once actually attached to the guide whilst in a life on earth, is *not really who they are*, but rather a reference point by which the sitter on earth may identify with them or call on them when in need. Sometimes guides will choose for themselves a name which they consider to be a pleasing phonetic arrangement of sound that will be acceptable to both guided and guide, but always it is a *reference label only* and not a permanent name attached to the spirit offering it. They don't, in fact, have or need one. Neither, eventually, will you. Two members of my spiritual 'team', as an example, have been referred to simply as 'The Big Indian' and 'The Persian Gentleman' for as long as I have worked with them during this incarnation, with these simplistic 'names' being quite acceptable to the two gentlemen as reference points that allow them to be identified in earthly terms when visiting me.

Sometimes, instead of a name, guides will give a sitter an image of an object – a feather or a rock, for instance – saying that whenever they think of the object in meditation they will be in contact with that guide. Should a guide prefer not to give you a name this does not make them any more difficult or easy to contact than any other guide. Should you need them, simply think of any description you have been given of them, or of any concept of them that you have built up in your mind and contact will instantly be made.

For quite different reasons (and also for the same ones if they are, in fact, highly evolved souls) family members communicating clairvoyantly with a sitter sometimes do not give their names. In any mediumistic session there is only a certain amount of time during which clairvoyance and clairaudience can take place. Eventually the medium tires, energies dip and the link has to be closed down. The vibrations that allow communication to take place, created from the higher side of life, can only be maintained for a given time too, and there are many other factors which can affect the duration of effective communication between differing worlds of consciousness (vibration) via a medium. People wishing to communicate from the spirit side of life 'queue up' mentally to speak through a medium (*also see How Mediumship Works, page 53*) and there is only so much available time during which any one spirit can talk to a sitter (often I am faced with several people from spirit trying to communicate at once, or cutting across each other in their eagerness to get through to the person on earth). For the people coming through, proving that they exist is absolutely the *last* thing on their agenda – they don't *need* to prove they exist – they *know* they exist. They will not waste precious time proving who they are (it is down to the medium to describe who he or she is seeing) when they only have a small 'window of opportunity' in which to make contact with the sitter, comment on the sitter's life and give them comfort, advice or reassurance.

Further, although mediums pick up sensations of 'hearing' the people who are communicating clairaudiently with them from the spirit worlds, these communicants are, in actual fact, *thinking* their intended messages towards the medium. The medium picks up the communication as speech but it is, in reality, *thought*. There is no need to vibrate the air between two people in the spirit worlds in order to communicate, or to move one's lips. Images and concepts are passed directly from mind to mind. Communicators will, therefore, as an option to giving a name, sometimes project to the medium a vision of where they once lived or mentally produce a picture of some object that was of great personal importance to them whilst on earth and is known to both communicator and sitter.

Frequently, when time allows and energies are high, names *are* given. Sometimes, however, the medium's description of the person, plus the personal images generated by the communicator from spirit, must suffice. I always explain to a sitter that they can check up on the person afterwards from the medium's description of the communicator if they have not been given a name – and that it is not actually *who* the communicator is that is important at the time of a reading (unless a communicator has come through with the specific intention of proving that they are all right and still exist in order to dispel grief in the sitter) but *what they are saying* to the sitter about the sitter's life and circumstances that is of greatest significance.

We tend, as sitters, to get sidetracked and bogged down at times by *who* the messenger is, when it is *the message itself* we should be paying most attention to.

Question: Do angels exist and what do they look like? Do they have wings?

A. I have been privileged on a number of occasions during my work as a medium to have been visited by angels. These ethereal beings 'feel' quite different in nature when compared vibrationally to the human souls we usually communicate with during clairvoyant work – their energy 'signature' radiating great spiritual power, purity and order. When seeing angels clairvoyantly I suddenly become aware of a change in the intensity of the communication 'field' emanating from the higher side of life, sensing a new communicator who is somehow so much grander in scale than any human soul. Although angels can be seen in their entirety clairvoyantly one feels dwarfed by their presence, as though their light and aura extends far beyond the limits of what mediumistic vision is capable of conveying. There is a sense of massive presence and vast dimensions that cannot easily be explained in earthly terms, together with a feeling of absolute permanence, about an angel's vibration, as though they always were and always will be what they are, unsullied by the earth plane, which they are never destined to incarnate into.

Please don't misunderstand me – I am not putting down in any way the highly evolved and luminescent human souls who regularly communicate with me and other mediums on behalf of others on earth. These human teachers and guides are every bit as glorious and spiritual as the angel messengers who occasionally choose to make their presence known. I am simply trying to explain that the human soul and the angel be-ing are two different aspects of creative – God – consciousness, with the human soul taking a path through many existences and experiences in order to evolve which the angel will never tread. Angels exist within a realm of heavenly light which is separate from, yet parallel to and interactive with, the many levels of consciousness available to the human soul. They are expressions of God Will given form and, acting within that Will, are the architects, builders and 'demolition experts' behind the changes that occur in this universe and others, those changes always being a part of that Divine plan to refine, evolve and distil matter into ever more ethereal expressions of God be-ing.

Intense, brilliant light emanates from every angel I have ever seen, and a variety of colours and combinations of colours stream from different angels. I have seen an angel clothed in a silver light that quickly filled my room until all I could see was silver; one surrounded by a deep, blood-red aura, and yet another clothed in multi-coloured streams of energy. Light pours out from the heart area of their being in all directions and seems to curve upwards and outwards at the back in living pulses of colour, giving the impression of wings and of even greater height. Their light is so bright that it is often difficult to see the human-like figure at its centre, just discernible through the overpowering radiance.

Sometimes a handsome/beautiful face can be seen, often in hues of gold and with golden hair, but I'm never quite sure whether the angel I'm communicating with is male or female, as their faces and voices seem to have characteristics of both sexes. On occasion they talk to me directly, with the voice being sensed rather than heard and again seeming powerful (and as though it is being purposely restrained or dampened in some way in order that communication can take place without harming the medium); sometimes they say nothing and I instead pick up silent impressions of what it is the angel wishes to pass on to the person they want to communicate with. After communication has taken place it invariably takes me some hours to 'come back to this world' mentally and physically (for my vibration to slow down to the point where I am operating fully in this level of consciousness again) so other-worldly is their presence and so powerful its effect on my mind and soul.

We may not realise it, but *each of us* has an ongoing link to one of these majestic beings and is angelically protected throughout the journey that is our physical life. Not only is every one of us assigned various spirit guides, we are also under the protection of an angelic being, a heavenly guardian who has never been polluted by the heavy vibrations of earth via incarnation into physical life. Just as angels work behind the scenes to manifest the intentions of God on a universal level, they also work as a channel for Divine intent with regard to human progression, ensuring that each individual soul is shielded from anything that is not intended to happen to it along its karmic path and that it is also protected whilst experiencing the life lessons it is here to learn from. The feeling that you should not go down a certain street on a certain day, for example, or the inner prompting that makes you take a right turn rather than a left one for no apparent reason, or the disembodied voice that suddenly cries *stop* and prevents you from stepping into the path of some oncoming vehicle often has as its origins the guiding love of a guardian angel.

You, personally, have assigned to you by God your own guardian angel who will be with you throughout your earthly life. Unseen, your angel links to you night and day to ensure that, whatever ills may appear to befall you on earth, the minimum of disturbance is caused to your soul in spiritual reality. Your angel guardian is able to protect you on all levels of life, within the karmic bounds of what your life has in store for you and, of course, depending on your own decisions to hear or ignore that inner voice. As I write I can sense tears from one of these great beings who is currently inspiring me – tears shed for the times when certain of us take decisions that plunge us into darkness and confusion for a time. During such episodes the guardian angel can only send out love and stand by, powerless to do anything for their charge until that soul makes a conscious decision to align itself with the light once more.

Your guardian angel works dispassionately on your behalf; that is to say, without the excesses of earthly emotion that seem to cause us all so much trouble. Does this mean that your angel is incapable of loving you and is a being of pure logic rather than one of love and compassion? As you can see by the reference to angel tears earlier, not at all. God *is* love – pure love untainted by the passions and biases and the wildly swinging emotions of the earthly mind. Angels are embodiments of and conduits for that Divine love energy, able, without being influenced by earthly passions or desires, to help the soul under their care steer a course back to God. Because they *are* love, every action they undertake on your behalf is born out of love. Your angel cannot help but love you. The challenges of earth that upset and disturb you so much are seen by the angel for what they actually are, opportunities to make you more God-like and to take you one step closer to home, to a joyful reunion with your Father. Your angel can therefore help you through them without becoming immersed in them or affected by them.

To an angel, guiding a human soul is a sacred trust. Your angel regards you as a precious jewel that has been given into their keeping for a time. They are the dedicated trustees of that jewel. Through an angel's eyes you are a light sent out into the darkness, a spark of God essence, an infant of God submerged in dense matter. The angel has the capability of seeing right through the illusion of that matter and, at all times, can see the soul on its journey for what it really is. The angel is an embodiment of God in the ethereal shepherding home an embodiment of God in the physical – you, their precious jewel.

Your angel is always there, close to you, patiently waiting for the God-child in its care to reawaken to the reality of spiritual life and an inner knowledge of its own heritage. As well as protecting you, the guardian angel's purpose in being with you is to surround you with gossamer fine spiritual energies that maintain your soul's sub-conscious connection with its heavenly roots, keeping you 'afloat' during your journey through earthly life, so that you do not sink so far into the seductive illusions of this earth that you completely submerge in them and forget, on a sub-conscious level, who you are and why you are really here.

It is such a pity that the sceptical nature of the human mind and the heavy vibrations of the earth plane so often conspire to mask the glorious light and steadfast love of the guardian angel. You can, however, learn to reach out and contact your angel if you wish. Begin by acknowledging their presence. By talking to them. By sending them your love each day. By asking them to help with your problems. By inviting them to make their involvement in your life known. If you are very quiet and still and trusting and can truly let go of your earthly problems and cares for a few moments each day you may then begin to sense your angel's presence as a golden mist or a very gentle and delicate warmth around you in times of meditation or when you are outdoors connecting with nature. You may also feel your angel's presence as a gentle steadfastness emanating from a being you will sense around you who feels to be of a finer, more ethereal vibration than the usual human spirit visitors.

With patience, you will begin to sense an almost child-like joy from an unseen someone at your side. A playful innocence that delights in your company. A quiet knowing that everything is all right in your life, and that you are not, in reality, lost or in trouble or alone, despite what outer appearances may tell you. You may also sense the presence of someone who is communicating with you not through words, but through vibrations of love and support – someone who, no matter where you are or what you are doing, is a constant, uncritical and loving companion.

Question: How does mediumship work?
What happens on this and the higher side
of life during a clairvoyant session to
allow communication to take place?

A. Mediums are 'put together' as spiritual and physical be-ings in a slightly different way than most people are. That is to say, their physical minds and bodies and higher minds and bodies are not bound as tightly together during their earthly journey as they are in the majority of human beings. Mediums, therefore, tend to live their lives with one foot in this world and one foot in the next, so to speak, which often accounts for our eccentricity and extreme sensitivity when measured against the way society expects people to behave! This loose and flexible connection between the physical and the etheric in our make-up is a major factor in the process that allows mediumistic souls to see, hear and interact with people wishing to communicate through them from a finer or higher vibration of matter.

Usually human beings cannot interact with – cannot see, hear or sense – spirits who may wish to contact this level of consciousness because the vibration of the souls desiring communication is faster than ours, rendering them invisible and inaudible to the coarser earthly senses. When a medium wishes to work clairvoyantly, his or her vibration automatically 'speeds up' (or, to be more precise, the rate of vibration at which their *spirit body and soul* normally operate speeds up) as they turn their will to the business of spirit communication. The medium's spirit self – the real 'them' – then takes the vibrational equivalent of a 'side step' out of the physical body as they open up (again, usually automatically) their main spiritual energy centres (*chakras*). Having made this adjustment in consciousness the medium is connected temporarily to both the physical *and* spiritual worlds, and is able to receive information via the chakras from both levels of vibration at the same time. As the medium connects in this way the guides working with them form a living conduit between this world and the next by mentally channelling through and slowing down the vibrations of the people on the spirit side of life who wish to communicate through the medium. The vibratory rates of the medium's spirit (having speeded up) and the communicating spirits (having been slowed down by the guides) synchronise for a time and communication – seeing, sensing and hearing on a higher level of consciousness (or multiple levels if the medium is communicating with a mix of family members, guides and, occasionally, angels) is then possible for the medium. *

The medium's 'team' of spirit workers has very distinct and particular functions to perform when working with and through their earthly instrument. A medium will always have what is called a doorkeeper guide present whenever he or she is operating mediumistically. The function of this particular spirit is, in earthly terms, to stand firmly in the 'doorway' between the two worlds, between the medium and the spirits who are wishing to emanate – to communicate – through that medium, and to act as an energy barrier to protect the medium's psyche. Consider that a medium's mind is willingly open to outside influences from the spirit world whenever they work for the light. Not all spirit influences are positive ones and not all spirit worlds are realms of light. (*Also see entry on Spirit Possession, page 89.*) Should the doorkeeper feel that harm is about to come to the medium, either from the vibrations of certain of the spirits wishing to use the medium, from the intentions of less evolved spirits who may be lurking in the background, or via something certain spirits might reveal to the medium if allowed to make contact with them, then the doorkeeper guide will immediately shut down the link between the medium and the spirit world in order to protect their instrument.

In addition to doorkeepers, there are also guides who act as organisers of communication on the spirit side of life, who take out the call to the people in spirit who wish to talk to their loved ones whilst there is an opportunity to do so through a medium. These guides arrange the souls wishing to communicate in some kind of order so that the medium does not receive a confusing cacophony of voices and images from a number of spirits at the same time. I can often feel the eagerness of the spirit people who wish to talk through me during a clairvoyant session, and, occasionally, two or three souls do 'jump the queue' and vie for attention at the same time. Without a guide to operate a kind of spiritual 'crowd control', clairvoyance would be much more difficult than it already is!

Finally, a number of power-building guides work around mediums at the same time as the doorkeeper and communicant – co-ordinating guides are carrying out their duties. Their function is to raise the vibrations – the energies – surrounding and interpenetrating the medium by creating a 'bubble' of high vibrational energy around their instrument within which communication can take place between the spirit worlds and the earth plane. Within that bubble (which distances the medium to some degree from the coarser vibrations of the earth plane whilst spirit communication is taking place) they maintain high and pure energies around their instrument for the duration of the communication. The bubble is an extremely delicate, etheric structure, and can be disrupted very easily from the earth side of life. It is therefore of paramount importance during any clairvoyant demonstration to refrain from unwrapping sweets, chatting to each other, answering your mobile phone or leaving the room to visit the bathroom!

When the level of energy required for communication can no longer be maintained, or when all intended communication has taken place, the bubble is instantly de-constructed and the link with the spirit side of life is withdrawn. The point at which this occurs may or may not coincide with the desired time scale of the people gathered on earth for the purpose of spirit communication – i.e. the desired length of a reading or the scheduled end time of a demonstration taking place in a church – but when the energies are withdrawn by the guides that is the end of communication on that particular occasion and the medium has no choice but to call an end to the demonstration.

When the time allotted for communication by the spirit world comes to an end the medium will either sense that the level of spiritual power has 'dropped' or suddenly be confronted by the fact that the team has shut down the energy bridge and that all clairvoyant activity has abruptly ceased. At this point the medium will usually feel drained and a little disorientated, and should be given time to shut down his or her chakras (so that he or she is no longer receiving images from outside of him/herself) and for his or her vibration to slow down again so that they can function normally in this world. It is not a good idea to bombard a medium with questions or requests for further clairvoyance following a demonstration as, believe me, they will feel depleted and tired, will involuntarily pick up your vibrations if they have not fully shut down yet, and all they will really want to do is have a quiet cup of tea and go home!

I remember, when first developing my mediumistic gifts, that dialogue from the spirit world seemed to stream past me at lightning speed, and at first I was only able to pluck the odd word out of the communication as it flashed by. As I became used to my vibration changing up a gear in frequency I was able to tune in to what was being said, and to see who was saying it, with increasingly efficiency.

Question: What is karma?

A. Karma, quite simply, is your single most important reason for being here on earth.

Tell me – how long is it since you left school? Perhaps you walked out of those iron gates for the final time twenty years ago – or perhaps only yesterday. On the other hand you may still be looking forward to that last day of that last term... *ever*. If you have already left your school days behind you how do you now look back at those times? With fondness, perhaps? Or were you relieved to finally escape from what you considered to be ridiculous constraints and to enter the 'real world' where you could at last make your own decisions and do things your way? Ladies and gentlemen, I have news for you – *not one of us ever leaves school* – not from cradle to grave as we move through this level of consciousness. You are in school *right now* as you read this; whoever you are, wherever you are and whatever you do in life. Whether you are at work at this moment, or on holiday, or sitting at home on a sofa, *you are still in school*, spiritually speaking. The whole earth plane is one gigantic school complex, able to offer its pupils – incarnated souls of which you are one – wonderful opportunities to become *more* than they were when they were born into it... and all because of *karma*.

You have *willingly* enrolled in the earth school for a fixed term as a soul with a physical body in order to learn, to grow, to evolve, and to *become*; and your present life on earth will offer you, at certain intervals along its unfolding, lessons in that school that will *inevitably* come to you as perfect opportunities to achieve these goals. Each of these lessons is a vitally important milestone that your soul *will* reach at some point during your earthly life, and each lesson will immerse you in a specific set of circumstances that will play out around your soul so that you may quicken your vibration (evolve spiritually by making decisions and taking actions and thinking thoughts which en-lighten your soul) through the ways in which you tackle the unfolding challenges. These milestones are karmic – are *karma* – that is to say they are the tests or exams specifically formulated to allow you opportunities to grow whilst in school on earth. They happen to you with your permission, with your consent having been given before you came to earth, and with your memory of this now dimmed in order that the challenges be as effective as possible (what is the point in meeting exams you are totally familiar with in advance and, therefore, equipped to avoid?). Whatever else you do in life is, ultimately, unimportant from the point of view of your soul. It is the uplifting of your essence – through *karma* – that you are here to bring about.

Karma, then – those teaching milestones that you have brought with you to confront and to overcome during your life – is an opportunity – an *ongoing* opportunity. It is growth through cause and effect, if you like, a continual process that refines and evolves you through many individual existences and experiences, not just through the lessons of this present earthly chapter. To understand karma you have only to look at the things you are doing today. Anything you do – anything you put into your life physically and mentally within this twenty four hour period, from what you eat to what you think to where you go, will alter the outcome of and have some effect on what you will get out of your life tomorrow. The way you have lived your life today has changed you from who you were this morning when you rose from your bed. You have added to your experiences and your knowledge. You have begun certain things, carried certain situations forwards and ended others. At any point in your life you are the sum of your todays, and as they become your yesterdays they shape your tomorrows. Karma is the same law of cause and effect at work on a grand scale and is concerned with the expansion of your soul. You *are* a soul, of course, and the way that you as a soul affect the ether around you today (by your beliefs, your biases, your choices in thought, etc.) shapes the adventure that will happen to your soul tomorrow. Because you are a soul with an infinite existence you arrive here on earth with certain circumstances already built into your coming life that you will bring into existence at intervals within that lifetime because having already created them by your past choices and actions as a soul in other existences. You can liken being born on earth to entering a new year at school. You bring to that new year some knowledge – certain strengths and weaknesses from your past experience as a pupil that are already a part of your consciousness, and you enter that new year with certain learning experiences ahead of you that will build on your past performance as a pupil during earlier 'school terms'.

In spiritually minded circles we often talk glibly about good karma and bad karma, don't we? We infer that we, as souls, earn bonus points or store up punishments for ourselves depending on how we react to life's karmic lessons. Whilst this has some truth to it as a very broad analogy, karma should not be looked upon in so grim a way. The karmic process is not an unyielding sheepdog snapping at your heels to herd you in a specific direction and make sure you act in a perfect way all the time, but rather a benevolent travelling companion, a friend by your side offering you limitless chances to get to know yourself better, to refine yourself, to decide over time what you are and what you are not, to admit more God light into your consciousness.

Karma has been your companion since you first became individualised as a soul and began to express yourself in relation to other souls and to your God, and its effects and repercussions stretch across all of your existences. Sometimes spirit guides who come through to me on behalf of sitters explain why the sitter is experiencing certain circumstances in this present physical lifetime, referring those circumstances back to things the soul decided it wanted to learn this time around, or to lessons from past lifetimes that are still unfolding and playing themselves out in this current physical existence. (*Also see entry on Reincarnation, page 28.*)

There are no right or wrong ways – as we define the two concepts in earthly society – to tackle the karmic challenges that come to us, there are simply short cuts (vibrationally uplifting and refining consequences as a result of your actions and decisions within a karmic situation) or long paths (vibrationally restrictive circumstances as a result of your actions and decisions within a karmic situation) open to you dependent on the course of action you choose to take in any karmic circumstances. Approach a karmic lesson in one way and it will take you some considerable time to work your way out of its repercussions. Tackle it in another way and you will learn very quickly from its lessons, its circumstances will disappear from your life, and you will then move on to the next lesson.

But how, you may ask, can you learn from the karmic lessons you are here to experience when you don't know what those lessons are? It is relatively easy to see karmic patterns in your life if you know what to look for, and then to deduce from them the lessons you are here to learn. If you would like some insight into your karmic lessons make a cup of tea, sit down and take a quiet, unhurried look at your life to date very carefully. Examine the good times, of course, but more importantly, look at the 'bad' times. Look at the ways in which you have related to people and they to you. Look at the times when you have suffered loss or sorrow. Look at the times when things did not turn out as you had expected them to. Then, having done that, ask yourself this – have you ever found yourself in desperate or upsetting or challenging situations and eventually fought your way out of them, only to have them repeat themselves, to turn up again in your life like the proverbial bad penny, at a later date? Perhaps the players and the locations changed the second and third time around but essentially the situations were the same – remakes of, or sequels to the original with different actors and settings delivering the same themes? Have you ever said to yourself, "Here I am *again* – however did I get myself into such a mess again when I promised myself I wouldn't?" If you have (and I'd be surprised if you haven't) then y*ou are identifying a karmic situation.* Quietly ask yourself what those circumstances have been trying to teach you about yourself and others who relate to you and why they have come back into your life. If you have not learnt a karmic lesson effectively the first time around it will keep on manifesting around you at intervals *until you react to it in a different way.* Then the circumstances will evaporate as quickly as dew in the morning sun and you will move on to the other lessons your karma has in store for you.

Also be aware that your actions on a daily basis are creating *new karma* ahead of you all the time. As a broad example, years of purposely and willfully hurting people in word and/or deed will eventually and inevitably bring back to you circumstances in which you are hurt in a similar manner, so that you can experience the error in the ways you have acted and find a better, more spiritual way to react to others. Similarly, years of trying hard to love and to help people will bring back to you the love you have given out. Of course, our time here in a physical body is limited, so our karma at our time of passing is always a mixture of things achieved and things that have yet to be worked out in some future existence. In other words, our karma does not end once we leave the earth plane. We are ever striving upwards and, whether we choose to come back to earth, to experience a different existence, or to move onwards strictly within spiritual realms, karma will again be by our side guiding us towards circumstances that will eventually allow us to achieve our goals.

Karma applies not only to individuals, but also to groups of souls, to nations and to mankind as a species, and the geographical location and social circumstances into which you are born allow you to not only work out your individual karma but also to contribute to and benefit from the karma of the people who are around you in family, in friendship, in work circumstances and who relate you you indirectly on this level of consciousness as the other members of your nation. Karma is an intricate jigsaw puzzle of opportunity linking the whole of mankind in a poetic dance of limitless experience which will eventually bring enlightenment to every single soul on earth (the patterns of which can be clearly seen if you stand back far enough in meditation, or look back on humanity from the viewpoint of one of the high spiritual realms).

As an example of how karma embraces the whole as well as the individual within the whole, consider that often a handful of members from a group soul (*also see entry on Group Souls, page 67*) will incarnate in order to experience karmic lessons that have relevance to the desired spiritual advancement of the whole group and may not have been instigated by the past actions of the individuals from the group choosing to visit the earth. This is allowed so that the volunteers who have incarnated on earth from that group soul may help refine *the whole group* through the karmic experiences they undergo whilst still on this level of consciousness.

Because we are all linked, because we are all part of the same thing, we share, to a lesser or greater extent, the consequences and rewards of karma on a number of different levels. It therefore follows that, as we evolve individually through the opportunities our own personal karma brings us, we influence to varying degrees the karma and therefore the spiritual evolution of those souls immediately linked to us and, ultimately, the karma of all souls everywhere.

Question: What is a group soul?

A. How similar are you and your close friends in outlook, personality and interests? Some of them will be very like you, of course, whilst others probably couldn't be more different. However alike or dissimilar you and each of your friends may be as personalities, there will be some common ground within your friendships. There will be points within each friendship at which there is a meeting of minds, at which your soul and the soul of your friend seem to dovetail together perfectly like two interlocking jigsaw puzzle pieces. There will be themes or outlooks common to you both that give you both a special pleasure when you acknowledge, share and explore them in each other's company. You form and maintain friendships because you discover a harmonic agreement between yourself and certain individuals regarding specific ideas, opinions, pastimes, outlooks, tastes, etc., and this harmony, when celebrated in friendship, *brings you a sense of pleasure and fulfilment* you would miss were those friendships not in place. Throughout your life you therefore make conscious distinctions between casual acquaintances and friends. Some relationships you maintain on a polite intellectual basis only; with others you let down the barriers and choose to include those select individuals within your more private life experiences. From that point of inclusion onwards they are your friends, however frequently or infrequently you may actually see them and, whether you admit it or not, you actually love them to some degree. Your friendships do, of course, also offer you many other benefits, such as the advice, support, comfort and companionship we all need at times as we journey through our physical lives.

If you are married or living within a one to one loving relationship, the two of you will have first been attracted to each other and then grown towards each other because of certain harmonies you both felt on a far more intense – a deeper – level than you allow yourselves to experience with other people. In all harmonic relationships, whether intimate marriage/love partnerships or close friendships, your reason for including the people you choose to be with in your life is because they bring an extra dimension – a special quality and richness – to your existence.

Why should things be any different once we return to the spirit side of life? That fuller existence, just like this fleeting one, is a continuing journey of experience and the phrase 'no man is an island' is even more valid when applied to the companionship needs of men and women on the spirit side of life. You see we are not, at spiritual heart, individuals at all, but in reality an integral part of each other and of God. True, we need silence and contemplation, inner communion and personal space in order to find ourselves and to experience God, both here and in the next worlds, but we also find God in the harmonious contributions others make to our lives and we to theirs. Our friends are like mirrors held up to ourselves – in them we see favourable aspects of ourselves (and, at times, unfavourable ones too!) reflected back at us. As we progress spiritually, we increasingly appreciate the joy of having like–minded souls around us. In the spirit realms we therefore gravitate, subconsciously at first and then, later, consciously, towards people who are of a similar spiritual outlook – who have spiritual goals identical to our own in mind.

As we journey through the spiritual spheres the harmony – the integration of purpose, intention, appreciation and respect – between numbers of us as souls grows stronger, until we eventually discover that we have gravitated towards a group of people on the spirit side of life with whom we can totally share our outlook and our goals and who want to move forwards into greater experiences of God and, perhaps, to undertake specific spiritual projects, in exactly the same way we do. At this point – this realisation of an inclusion within the extended, harmonious family of beings that is the group soul – there may also be an awakening to the fact that many of these people are souls we have known and shared existences with before; that they are part of a group soul we have 'belonged to' for some considerable time without being aware of that truth. We will realise that we are, from this moment in our spiritual journey onwards, able to work and to evolve and to socially and spiritually interact with these people as a conscious part of the group, knowing that from now on our karma and destiny are so closely bound up with the karma and destiny of this group of souls as to be one and the same thing. (*Also see entry on Karma, page 59.*)

This does not mean that we will at some point give up our individuality of consciousness, outlook or privacy in order to become a member of a group soul. It simply means that we will acknowledge and delight in something within each member of that group soul that joyfully binds us to them, them to us, and every soul within the group to every other member of that group. It is a tie that binds not through restriction but through recognition and love and unity of purpose.

Allow me share with you some small insight into the state of *be-ing* – into the way of life – of a group soul...

Many years ago, whilst sitting one afternoon in meditation with the lady who helped me develop as a medium, I was suddenly surrounded by a number of the guides who work in the team of which she and I are a part. "Don't be afraid," was their rather odd first statement to me that day. "I'm not," I replied, wondering what was about to happen. "Don't be afraid," they repeated. I could feel power quickly building in the room and knew something special was about to happen.

I looked down and realised that I had left my physical body and, still surrounded by the guides from the team who had formed a protective circle around me, seemed to be hovering not in the living room of a small house in Lancashire but, curiously, over a patch of perfect green grass. "Don't be afraid," they repeated once more. I looked down again, still at the centre of this circle of friends, and discovered that I was now hundreds of feet up in the air. On earth I am terrified of heights to the point of almost losing consciousness if I am somewhere elevated with no supportive structure around me, but in spiritual environments the things that worry you on earth seem to melt away as you realise no harm can come to you, and I felt quite calm and secure despite the circumstances.

Below me sprawled the most wondrous and colourful landscape I have ever seen. Perfect fields formed a patchwork of greens and russets and yellows. A river of pure silver light, as still as a mirror, threaded its way through the countryside, and on it I could see people in small boats enjoying themselves. I looked ahead and to each side and found that all around me this landscape spread out, completely flat and without any curvature, to the far distant horizons. In the distance ahead of me I could see what I can only describe as a city, although it was like no city on earth. It seemed to be composed of shimmering crystal buildings, and shafts of multi-coloured light energy descended from the heavens into the heart of this place.

I looked up into the cloudless sky (there was no sun, yet everywhere was bathed in a perfect sunlight) and saw streaks of brightly coloured light shooting towards me and tearing past me at lightning speed. At first I was puzzled as to what these heavenly lights could possibly be, then it became obvious as the streaks passed close to me that they were, in fact, *people* in coloured spirit robes flying over this perfect landscape, travelling from point A to point B by willing themselves to their destinations at the speed of thought. No need for cars or aeroplanes in this place! The coloured streaking effect was caused by the phenomenal speed at which they travelled, with them leaving the spiritual equivalent of a vapour trail behind them.

As I marvelled at this phenomena the guides prepared me mentally for a 'landing' and, looking down, I saw my feet touch down gently on another area of soft, perfect grass.

Around me, and at various locations upon the landscape, stood members of a group of individuals who I psychically sensed were working together at some complex task beyond my comprehension. They were dressed in identical spirit robes of exactly the same hue and, although they were definitely individuals, there was a mental and spiritual unity of purpose that could be felt emanating from these souls. Catching my attention one of them gestured to a boulder, about the height of a tall man, that stood upon the grass. Telepathically he made me understand that this rock was regarded by the group as an integral part of the group soul, and acknowledged as being of equal value to the human souls in the group. In other words, these souls were in absolute harmony with the amazing landscape around them and had evolved and matured spiritually to the point where they not only knew as fact that all expressions of creation are alive, but also regarded all the different aspects of their living environment to be as much a part of the group soul as they were. The *landscape itself* was treated as a part of the group soul.

I could have stayed forever in that carefree atmosphere of love and harmony. Here conflict and war simply did not exist and there was an air of permanence about everything. Here one knew in one's heart that nothing decayed as it did on earth. Unfortunately my guides intimated that it was time to go and, after a sensation of falling into myself, and of there being 'two of me' (the spiritual and the physical) for a moment, I reluctantly found myself once more in my body, sitting in an armchair in a living room in the north west of England. To this day I have never forgotten that small peek into the harmonious world of a group soul operating on a level of consciousness that, in earthly terms, my guides informed me, was just two levels above this one. What unimaginable glories are waiting for us as we eventually, as members of group souls, travel to the higher vibrations beyond that amazing world, I wonder?

I had met only a handful of the complete membership of that group during my brief excursion to the realms of light, and such a group in its entirety can total thousands of souls. As a group soul moves further into the heaven worlds, it eventually merges with other group souls to form even larger families of consciousness and spiritual purpose, which eventually merge with other groups and so on. We are all on a journey home to God and, as we slowly grow closer to our destination, we grow closer to each other. We do not lose our identities. Instead those identities – those aspects of us that make us uniquely *us* – are cherished and revered within the groups we will eventually become a part of for the qualities they will bring to the group's consciousness and experience.

Question: Do you believe God exists?
If so, how do you perceive God?

A. I never fail to be shocked when either a sitter or someone in a spiritualist church asks me if I believe in God. I'm shocked because, whilst many people are prepared to believe in a spirit world, and in a life after physical death, and to seek out clairvoyance and mediumship, and to sing hymns in a church where mediumship takes place, not all of them are prepared to believe in a creator.

Yes, I believe in God. From the beginning, my experiences working as a medium drew me not only to the inevitable conclusion that God exists, but also to realise that nothing *outside* of God r*eally exists at all*, except in the minds of men and women. In other words, not only is there a God, there is *only* God. The whole of creation *is* God and is contained *within* God – and the only barrier to us realising that fact and to living more fulfiling lives is the negativity and evil and intellectual arrogance we create for ourselves on this level of consciousness (and on the lower astral plane beyond this one).

I have discovered and have been shown repeatedly that *everyone and everything* is a manifestation of God... Many years ago I was sitting on a bench in my back garden one hot summer's evening relaxing. As I looked at the plants in front of me, not really seeing them, suddenly one of the spirit guides who works with me popped up behind the bench and said, "Look at the grass." A little startled I dutifully looked at the lawn and could see nothing out of the ordinary. "Look at the grass," the guide repeated, more insistently. I looked at the patches of green again and this time switched over to clairvoyant vision. I then began to see a pattern of blue-white light flowing through every blade of grass in the garden. "Now," said the guide. "Look at the stones." I looked at the rocks and stones in that garden with mediumistic eyes and within them I could see the same light. The patterns the light was forming were slightly different than those I could see in the lawn, but the quality and intensity of light was identical to that streaming through the grass. "Now," said the guide. "Look at the fence." I turned my attention to the fence and saw the same light quality, again in a slightly different pattern, pulsing through the wooden slats that made up the boundary of my garden. I then glanced at my hands and my forearms as they rested on my knees and saw an identical vibration of light streaming through them. Wherever I looked in that garden that evening I could see objects ablaze with the same blue-white light and with dancing patterns of light energy. My guide had shown me something I had long suspected to be true – that we are all made up of the same building blocks – that we are all part of the same thing, part of each other, part of creation, part of *God*. It was God energy I was witnessing that evening – alive, vibrant, shaping and maintaining in their patterns and forms the various aspects of creation in that garden, from the plants to my physical body.

You see, the statement 'we are made in God's image' is only a pale representation of the truth. Each of us is far more than a mere copy, a reflection of, the Divine. Each and every one of us actually *is* a *fragment* of the Divine, a true son or daughter of God; a facet – a spark – of God be-ing given the illusion of separateness and sent out on an amazing adventure so that we might grow and so that God might experience aspects of His creation through our unique approach to and perceptions of physical and spiritual life. Not only is each one of us a part of God, everything we relate to via our physical and spiritual senses is *also* a part of God, from a teacup to an armadillo; from a length of steel pipe to a rose; from a piece of music to a distant star. At its core everything, *everything* is *alive* and is made in God's image, because everything is contained within and issues from the infinity of God consciousness.

There is a tendency with some souls who are trying to develop the spiritual gifts to elevate spirit guides to the level of importance and capability of God, almost worshipping them as infallible beings and praying to them rather than to the source. This is both wrong and dangerous, and your guides would be the first to tell you so. I never go to guides for advice or guidance except having first prayed to God – aligned myself in consciousness with Him – so that anything that comes to me in the way of help or inspiration or advice manifests with His permission and along His perfect vibration. By doing this I protect myself from any lower, lesser vibrations (there is no higher vibration than that of

God consciousness) and any negative or devious emanations from the minds of unenlightened souls that might otherwise attempt to influence my consciousness during periods in which my chakras are open to admit information and images from other levels of be-ing.

So – who or what, exactly *is* this God I approach so regularly in prayer and talk to constantly and who I am so sure exists?

Don't expect a complicated answer, because God is simply That Which Is.

We, as his beloved children, are simply that which proceeds from That Which Is.

If you would gaze upon the face of God you need look no further than into the eyes of your partner or your child, or to look at the face of anyone and everyone you will ever meet. I am talking to God when I talk to you and I am looking at God when I look at you or observe my features in a mirror.

I believe that everything that is other than mankind – than the human – in the physical universe, and in the realms beyond it, is also God. From a sunset to a fruit fly, an angel to a ray of light, everything emanates from and is an expression of that one source of life. This doesn't mean that everything has the same degree of sentience – consciousness and self awareness – that we have as human souls, but God consciousness – intelligence – does flow through everything, because everything is composed of God energy. The universe is therefore alive and responsive and an integral part of us and requires our respect and our love.

Knowing this, knowing that we are a part of God and of each other and of everything else – truly realising and embracing this within our souls and our consciousness – alters forever the way we treat ourselves, the way we treat others and the way we treat this planet and its other, non-human citizens.

For example, if I lash out at you, or speak out against you, or envelop you in dark thoughts, I am harming God and, ultimately, because you are a part of me, I am harming myself too.

If I steal from you, or covet your land or your possessions, I am really stealing from God and therefore from myself.

If I stub out a cigarette on the earth, I am disrespectful of – am harming – the spirit that this planet, as a manifestation of God, really is, and am therefore also harming and disrespecting myself.

You may ask what proof I have for the existence of this all-embracing God energy that flows through and lies behind (with the exception of our own negativity) every aspect of this earth and beyond...

Other than personal experiences such as the one that took place in my garden, *none*, as the scientist on earth would measure physical evidence – but then scientists as a rule (and I'm sure there are exceptions) mostly concern themselves with the physical universe only. Anything they are unable to see, touch, feel, hear or smell on a basic physical level cannot, to their way of thinking, exist. I simply *know* as a soul that God exists. This is very different from *believing* He exists because I have been told this the case by a religious group. *Believing* is a mental exercise – *knowing* is an ongoing experience that manifests in your soul, that you feel as a constant at the point of your solar plexus, whatever the wavering physical mind may tell you day to day. *Knowing* means you can relax. The truth is there within you and it doesn't have to be worked at or taken out and consciously examined periodically or bolstered up or questioned. You *believe* with your physical mind – you *know* with your soul. I *know* God exists despite the shortcomings of my physical mind, because the knowledge comes from that deeper place within me which is Divine.

If you want to know and experience God, go within. Meditate regularly. Become quiet. Still your worries, your fears, your prejudices, your angers and the thousand and one jarring and distracting cacophonies of this physical world. Turn off the television for an hour – I dare you! Turn off the car radio. Turn off the computer. Turn off the demands of your physical body and your physical mind for a time and **Be Still**. Then, and with patience as you regularly visit that quiet place within you, you will begin to hear or to sense the still, small voice. You will experience a true communion that will fill you with peace and joy and, from that moment onwards, you will *know*.

Once you experience the reality of the God within you; once you understand – *know* – that there is nothing but God, and that the only barrier to discovering God and communing with Him lies in the illusions created within the human mind with its negativities and fears and the complicated mental arguments we invest so much time and energy into, you will become a better communicator, a better healer, a better medium, a better *person*. You will be able to call on that God power that is within you every day and allow it to manifest through every situation in your life, knowing that it will never, can never, *ever* fail you. The trials and challenges of your life won't go away, of course (*also see entry on Karma, page 59*) but you will find that you now approach them from a different perspective, knowing that everything in your life is working to the good and that you are never alone in whatever circumstances you face.

Rejoice! God exists, *you* are a part of Him and, there is nothing – *ever* – to fear.

Question: Why does God allow – or, worse still, cause – wars and natural disasters to happen? How can these events be due to the actions or inactions of a loving God?

A. That God allows wars and natural disasters to happen cannot be in doubt. Otherwise He would intervene whenever we were in danger from imminent violence – either manmade or natural – and He most certainly does not do this. Is His lack of action in such matters to therefore be taken as the mark of an unloving and indifferent God? Or, worse still, could we all be at the mercy of a vengeful God who actually causes and wants these awful disasters to happen to the world and to us in some way? A resounding *No!* on both counts! God's seeming inaction (as in lack of *interference*) has to do with the old chestnut of *free will*. God has created us as His children, not His puppets. True love does not seek to control or to coerce. Although we are a part of Him we have been given absolute freedom of choice in our lives. Within the limits imposed on us not by God but by human society, we are free to exercise that free will – to go wherever we like, to do whatever we like and, most importantly, to *think* whatever we care to think. Of course, we do all these things with great gusto, using our free will, in many cases, to make a complete and utter mess of our lives and the lives of others as we proceed along life's path. When things subsequently go wrong for us we waste no time in conveniently blaming the harvest of our own actions on our God.

Wars and natural disasters are opposite sides of the same coin. From a spiritual perspective they are inseparable, with one inevitably leading to the other. Consider this – there is a far more potent and destructive form of waste product poisoning this planet in the twenty first century than the air pollution, water pollution, noise pollution and other physical, man-made nasties we hear about so regularly in the news. This is the destructive vibrational effluent created minute by minute *by our own thoughts* – a pollutant we pour unceasingly into the earth's atmosphere and tissue and soul, day after day, night after night, not realising that this planet is a sensitive, receptive, living being just as we are. It nurtures us whilst we are here, providing the air we breathe and the food we eat and is deserving of our respect and love at all times. Unfortunately many of us at best refuse to acknowledge the importance of mother earth to us and at worst choose to harm her daily through our thoughts and actions.

We are spirit beings first and physical beings second. Our thoughts are the *living* creations of spirit beings and, as such, they have force and power and purpose and intent and *energy*. When our thoughts are eventually put into motion as physical action we are simply finally displaying manifestations of mental creations and intentions that can have been festering away – giving out power – on an etheric level for as long as we have been thinking them. The *moment* our thoughts are created they bring into being an unseen energy – either positive or negative, which not only affects the thinkers of those thoughts, but also emanates from their creators to affect – to impinge on – the energies of the immediate environment surrounding them. How many times have you psychically 'picked up' an atmosphere of despair or anger or malevolence in a house, long after the occupants who originally caused that disturbance have moved on? Our willful thoughts, *even if never followed up by any physical action*, radiate outwards from us taking with them the intent – the 'spin' – we have imbued them with mentally (anger, jealousy, depression, violence, etc.). These spreading thoughts first have an unseen affect on any people or situations they may be aimed at… more often than you think your uncharacteristic clumsiness – a predilection to bump into things and to unintentionally harm yourself – on certain days has been caused by your psychic interception and adsorption of thoughts being aimed at you by certain individuals who, for whatever reason, have take against you in some way. Unfortunately, radiating thoughts don't stop radiating once they have reached their intended target. The thoughts of mankind spread ever outwards from all of us to mingle with each other and to blanket the whole world. One person thinking negative and violent thoughts isn't going to harm the earth to any great degree, but consider how many millions of souls there are on this planet and the types of thoughts a great many of these souls give birth to, second by second…

What dominant thoughts *do* we, as individuals, as families and as nations, choose to pour into this beautiful planet's atmosphere from moment to moment? Loving thoughts, would you say? Harmonious thoughts, perhaps? Peaceful and constructive thoughts? If only these were the norm! Instead, many members of society elect on a daily basis to focus on hatred or thoughts of revenge; to nurture thoughts of violence or perversion; to launch thoughts of discord and disharmony into the world that supports their very existence. Many, many souls on earth seek to terrorise and to torture and to maim and to control and to manipulate, and the violent thoughts that proceed and interpenetrate these physical actions pollute and poison and weaken the structure of the earth day after day after day. Have we not been advised by the master spirits who have visited the earth at various times over the thousands of years that we have walked its surface that *love* should be the motive behind every aspect of our lives? Have we not been advised that love should be the guiding light behind everything we think, everything we say, everything we do? Have we heeded these words of spiritual wisdom, aimed at improving the lot of mankind as a whole and making each one of us happier and more fulfiled? Have we listened? Do we even *try* daily to be a little more loving in whatever small ways we can manage?

Instead our thoughts of revenge, of violence, of material acquisition at the cost of others, radiating daily from millions of minds, cluster together in intent and vibration (like attracts like, each thought seeking out and joining with others of its kind) building and becoming ever more powerful until they form an unseen force that bends and twists and stabs at the very fabric of this reality until something has to give. Is it any wonder, then, that the earth regularly rips itself apart and erupts in violence? Who do we then blame for this pitiful scream of pain from the the spirit that is this planet? "It's nothing to do with us," we cry! "How could God have done this to us? How could God have let this happen Why, God? *WHY*?"

We mistakenly believe we are separated from the forces of nature and are therefore at the mercy of them. In actual fact it is we who control the forces of nature via our thoughts. I'll say that again – *we are in control of the forces of nature* – albeit mostly subconsciously at this stage in our evolution as a species. We control them badly, but control them we do. Natural disasters are the end result of the law of cause and effect in action. Our thoughts are the cause – increasingly more violent worldwide disasters are the effect. Please don't take my word for this. Why not prove it to yourself by keeping a close eye on current events? Note down when every new war, every new skirmish, every new act of violence takes place. You will then begin to notice how, with alarming regularity, a short time after each major act of violence has been set in motion, the earth responds with a 'natural' disaster that is a direct reaction to the vicious mental attack we have just subjected it to. Our own violence is the instigator of the disaster in every case.

So – what can we do to stop this process from continuing? To finally change things for the better? How can you, as one small, insignificant individual, a tiny speck upon the face of the earth, make things more stable for yourself and for everyone else than they are at this present time? Firstly, by throwing out the idea that you are small, individual, insignificant and a tiny speck. *You are a part of God*, as equal and important a part of Him as any and every other soul on this earth. When you choose to align yourself with the forces of love and harmony you draw on true power, not the fleeting illusion of societal power, but the infinite, irresistible and unstoppable power of the God within you. You choose, though your God-given free will, to join forces with the powers of creation, not of destruction. You choose to live life on earth as God intends it to be lived, refusing to acknowledge (and therefore, refusing to give power – to give thought energy – to) or to indulge in the dominant desires of mankind for self-satisfaction and violence. By working daily to become a little more loving in whatever small ways you can manage, your soul becomes a channel for the light *at all times* in your life, so that you make a positive difference to every soul on this planet and to the planet itself, whether you are praying, actively meditating or simply watching your television or sleeping. Without you consciously being aware of the fact you will be used by higher forces, by guides and angels working on the instruction – the will – of God, a hundred times a day as an energy conduit to bring healing and harmonic power to your surroundings and to help restore a harmonic balance of being to this level of consciousness.

One day, when we fully understand and acknowledge our symbiotic link to the earth, we will control our weather systems and the natural forces around us quite easily and without technology simply by being more loving people, by sending out love and harmonic energies in groups, by understanding the awesome destructive or constructive power of our own thoughts and by realising that the earth is not separate from us at all, but an integral part of each of us and of God.

Question: Is there such a thing as spirit possession? Can an evil 'someone' or 'something' from the other side control or influence the actions and thoughts of a person on earth?

A. Part of my work as a medium over the years has involved me in visiting and 'clearing' households that are experiencing disturbance on a paranormal level.

In only a very small percentage of cases have I ever discovered something or someone malevolent behind the phenomena taking place, the disturbance usually being attributable to either a deceased person who has yet to realise that they have passed on and that they need to move forwards into the light and their new existence, or to family members in spirit who come back with something important to say to their relatives on earth – the occupants of the affected home – and, unable to make their presence known by clairvoyant means, find they can only attract attention to themselves by making noise or by moving objects on a physical level.

As stated, however, I *have* very occasionally found myself confronted in a disturbed house by malicious and troublesome spirits (who, I hasten to add, are subsequently no match for the guides in my team and are rapidly moved on by them). Further, I have also over the years been contacted on a number of occasions by distraught individuals who feel they are being controlled or influenced or 'taken over' to a lesser or greater degree by malevolent spirits and are experiencing phenomena as diverse as objects moving around their homes to physical sensations of being hit or pushed around and other manifestations of unseen aggression and menace.

So, to what extent *can* an unenlightened soul from the other side of life actually influence an individual on this level of consciousness and make their life a misery? Can they affect and influence their thoughts? Can they cause actual physical harm to someone? Can they force them to do things they don't want to do?

The short answer is – *only to the extent that the person on earth accepts and believes that they can and allows them to.*

There is no doubt that unenlightened spirits can and *do* sometimes decide to make someone's life on earth a misery and can have themselves a tremendously satisfying time upsetting someone *for as long as they are permitted to do so.*

Having first created an atmosphere of fear in the victim's mind (usually these souls are attracted to and link with their intended victims initially at a time during the person's life when they are vulnerable, tired, depressed or their spiritual defenses are down) they then use that fear – that apprehension in the mind – as a vibratory link to perpetuate their psychic bullying. As an analogy, if I tell you right now *not* to think of an elephant, what is the first thing you think of? Exactly! So it is with the irrational fear they create in the minds of their victims. Having been disturbed initially in some way by someone from the other side of life, the victim's mind repeatedly returns to the experience and to the fear that experience has caused them, strengthening and enhancing its power with every mental revisit to the original incident. Along that vibration of ever-increasing fear the unenlightened spirit can then reach the person again and again to cause further mayhem. The fear becomes a kind of permanently open telephone connection to the victim's consciousness.

Fortunately there are a number of things one can do to remedy such situations.

Firstly, the key to quelling the constant fear that 'something else is going to happen' lies in turning the mind completely away from any past incidents involving an unseen mischief maker, in refusing to entertain or give in to any thoughts of fear and disturbance and, in the case of spiritually gifted people who are under attack, in ceasing all activity that involves opening up the chakra energy centres or in undertaking any spiritual work until the link between the victim and mischievous spirit has been severed or sufficiently weakened to the point where the person on earth can deal with it and dispense with the psychic intruder. I always advise someone who is being plagued on a paranormal level to immerse themselves back into the illusion of this world *completely*. Not to attempt any kind of spiritual work whatsoever, nor to consider approaching spiritual subjects in mind or action, or to entertain any thought that there is a spiritual side to life, and certainly not to think about what has happened to them until the unwanted link has been severed. By concentrating solely on the sights, sounds and sensations of the earth plane the mind and psyche become fully occupied by the sensory demands of this illusion and are isolated from any conscious connections to the spiritual realms (as they are at birth until we actively seek them out again). The senses become totally caught up in the distractions of the earth level of consciousness, allowing the mischievous spirit no way in – no connection to its victim's mind.

The second mental course of action that can be taken when being pestered by a mischievous entity involves realising and affirming that *no-one from the other side of life can harm you unless you allow them to*; affirming constantly that the unseen 'friend' has no power over you, that their actions really don't bother you in any way, shape or form, and that there is 'only God' (*good*) and anything else is a lie – a falsehood. There is no fun in a game when the other person refuses to play, and any spirit delighting in causing mischief and mayhem soon moves on when the delight is taken out of their actions and no reward in the way of fear and upset is forthcoming from their victim. Aligning yourself constantly with God also brings the highest of protective vibrations around you, which no lower form of consciousness, no lesser rate of vibration, can penetrate.

Thirdly, and this is one of the most important factors in dealing with any negative influences from beyond this realm, we have to realise that our *motives* are our protection in life. If we have a obsessive predilection for drink or drugs, for example, or a strong wish to bring chaos and discord into other people's lives, or over-active sexual desires, then we really should not be surprised – considering that in spirit law like attracts like, thought-wise – if we attract the attention of some discarnate spirit who has a similar liking for the things we crave so much and have allowed to dominate our lives. This is not meant as a criticism or a judgement – it is simply an observation of the law of attraction in operation. Higher thoughts also come under this law, attracting the attention and involvement in a person's life of more spiritually enlightened souls – of workers for the light.

Many a poor alcoholic has suffered at the unseen hands of spirits goading them, via a psychic link, to take yet another drink. Many a drug taker has suffered at the hands of unenlightened and invisible tormentors and has been steadily and repeatedly pushed back in the direction of their habit. Why would certain spirits from the other side wish to do this to someone? The reasons, in these cases, are practical ones on the part of the discarnate spirit as some souls, upon leaving the earth, are loathe to also leave behind some of the physical sensations of this world, from tobacco to alcohol to drugs to sex to violence. The only way they can experience these sensations again – albeit second-hand – is by drawing close to someone on earth with a similar craving vibrationally and 'touching' their aura whilst the victim is enjoying the very sensation the discarnate spirit is seeking. Sensation transmitted unwittingly from the aura of the victim to the aura of the discarnate spirit allows the unenlightened soul to once again experience the sensations and lower emotions they have not yet learned to let go of, and so they goad and tempt their victims at a subconscious level to get what they want. Horrible, isn't it?

In similar vein consider the motives, on the whole, of people who approach the spirit world for the first time through a Ouija board. Isn't it true to say that these people – often youngsters – are looking for a thrill… a shock… something that will make the skin crawl on the back of their necks? *Like attracts like* and so, in most cases, they get exactly what they are seeking! You wouldn't go to bed and leave your front door unlocked and open and the house unprotected in this day and age, would you? And yet so many people do exactly this, spiritually speaking, when they use a Ouija board. They leave themselves open to the influence of any low spirits who wish to play the 'game'.

Don't do it, people! You don't know who you are talking to. They can tell you they are anyone – a great, exalted worker for God, for example, or an angel, but are you in a position to believe them when you can't actually see them and are approaching them without a doorkeeper and protective guides around you? (*Also see entry on How Mediumship Works, page 53.*) Highly evolved spirits will speak to you directly or through a medium – *never* through a Ouija board – and will *never* sing their own praises. Approaching the spirit world requires discipline and self control – you must know exactly what you are doing and who is contacting you at all times.

An old friend of mine still remembers, with chills flowing down his spine, the day when he and his then girl friend first approached the spirit world through a Ouija board. They were contacted by a spirit who at first seemed very plausible but gradually, in consecutive sessions with the board, began to control aspects of their lives, in the later stages of their dialogue even telling them to wear certain clothes with symbols on them, and where to buy them. Fortunately they had the good sense and fortitude to break free of this influence. Many have not been so lucky.

Many years ago, whilst just setting out on my spiritual work as a very green and impressionable medium and, I might add, at a time when I had just lost my father and was emotionally vulnerable, I met, through one of the spiritualist churches at which I was lecturing, a late middle aged couple who allegedly worked 'for the spirit' at a 'centre' they owned a few miles from the church. They also held healing sessions and weekends which mediums of some note would attend, 'living in' for a couple of days to give lectures and demonstrations. They were told that a new medium was lecturing at the church and that they really should attend.

At the end of the day I was introduced to the couple and invited to stay over at their 'centre' for a weekend to lecture to a number of guests. I eagerly accepted.

The couple lived in a large, old house surrounded by grassland. I didn't pick up any negative vibrations from the house – yet, in my defence, I was just starting out in this work and neither had any of the other reputable mediums who had visited and worked at the place. Over the next two days I gave my talks, plus a demonstration of clairvoyance. A number of guests were in attendance, including the daughter of the couple who had invited me there.

Some weeks later the daughter contacted me to arrange a personal reading. She proved to be a difficult subject – forthright, stubborn, inflexible and quite annoying. I passed on the messages I was given, however, and she seemed pleased with the results. She subsequently invited me to her home to give readings to five of her friends, and a further five readings were arranged for a future date. However, before this second appointment could take place the daughter rang me to see if I would like to go to a musical with her. At first (and reacting to my inner voice – though not strongly enough!) I very firmly said *no*. I then foolishly began to talk myself into going. "What harm could it do?" I asked myself. "I deserve a little time off, after all!" A couple of weeks later I found myself feeling quite uneasy as I sat next to the lady watching the musical. I have to say I didn't really find her attractive in any way and was relieved when the day was over and I was heading home. One interested thing *had* emerged during our conversations, however, concerning the fact that she, her mother and father and another gentleman regularly sat in a closed 'circle' to contact the spirit world around a table in a darkened room. I was told spirits talked to them through the table, either by rapping on it or by causing the table to move around the room. Not having witnessed physical phenomena at that stage in my work I was most intrigued. "Maybe we can fit you in on the evening you come to my house to do the readings," said the daughter. "I'll ask my mother and see what she says."

Surprise, surprise... mother said, "Yes."

I remember driving to the centre feeling buoyant about what was to occur, but also a little apprehensive. Following dinner we all moved into the small room in which I had slept when lecturing at the centre. In it was a bed, a wardrobe and a small, tall table shaped like an old fashioned threepenny piece. Chairs were positioned around

97

this and on it was placed a small decorated box which I later learned contained a number of tiny papyrus scrolls. Before the antics began, and with a pair of tweezers, the mother removed one of the scrolls, each of which contained a small quotation from the bible, and read from it. Curtains were then drawn, the light turned off and, in the pitch blackness as we sat around the table, the spirits were summoned.

I was asked to place my hands on the table as the others were doing. As my eyes grew accustomed to the dim light seeping in around the edges of the curtains I felt and saw this unremarkable piece of furniture lurch violently beneath my hands. The mother began to ask questions of the spirits present. Who they were, how they were – that type of thing. After each question the table would either heave about or spell out a message by tapping out a sequence of letters of the alphabet against someone's palm. Then something even more extraordinary happened. The table upturned itself onto my lap, the top sitting squarely on my knees, the legs pointing up into the air by my face. No-one from this world was touching it.

"Aaahhh," said the mother. "Look how it's sitting in Michael's lap. See how much affection they're bringing him from the spirit world!" I was feeling lonely and vulnerable, so despite – to say the least – the highly unusual circumstances it was comforting to identify with this 'loving embrace' that seemed to be directed to me via the table, which was exerting some considerable pressure on my legs.

I became a fairly regular visitor to these strange sessions, at first, in my naivety, seeing nothing wrong with them. I remember on one animated occasion the table fell over then dragged itself across to a wardrobe and pulled itself upright again using the other piece of furniture as a support.

Through this table I was regularly manipulated as a young, green and impressionable medium. Messages came through it telling me I would work at the house regularly and that the place was to become a worldwide centre – a beacon for the light and for the spirit and that I would play a vital part in that transformation. I was told that I and the daughter were soul mates (*also see entry on Soul Mates, page 22*), that we were to work together and to *marry*, and, for a time, even though I was in no way attracted to the daughter, I fell for what I was being told. Every time my own common sense kicked in and warned me that something was very wrong there would be another session with the table and I would be reassured by its manipulators that everything was perfectly all right and that I was simply adjusting to this new, glorious life of spiritual service that was stretching out in front of me.

Eventually, as this psychic snare tightened around me, there occurred a moment in which I began to question the right-ness of what was happening. One day the mother recounted how she had begun working with the table and quite matter of factly explained that *Jesus* had contacted her through it. She said he had told her that he would call her 'angel' and that she could call him 'Lord'. Hmmm, I thought, my stomach tightening. *What would Jesus want with a table?* Why would so elevated a soul choose that base method of spirit communication rather than, if he were truly there, just turning up and saying whatever he wanted to say to whoever he wanted to say it to?

Needless to say (and here I'm cutting short a long story that might, at some stage, become part of a future volume) I departed that situation at a rate of knots! So – what on earth (and in other dimensions!) was happening? The table actually moved – I repeatedly saw it do so. The entities communicating through it were obviously not who they seemed to be or said they were and the power of the minds of the people sitting around that table, having a certain purpose in mind – that of snaring me as a tame medium (a soon to be in-family source of income) for their glorious centre of light and marrying off their spinster daughter – were definitely contributing to the chaos. A cautionary tale, particularly for those of you actively pursuing a spiritual path through development of your gifts. Now, with years of experience under my belt, this type of situation is easy to spot and to avoid.

I cannot close this section without writing a few quick words concerning spiritual development circles. I have seen so many of these regular meetings of like-minded souls on earth who wish to develop their spiritual gifts set up with the highest of intentions, only to flounder and rip themselves apart due to jealousy and rivalry between members of the circle. Worse, I have seen members sitting in a circle attract, via the energy the circle radiates when in operation, confused and 'lost' spirits from the other side and unwittingly take them home with them, where these poor souls reside, unknowingly causing depression and unease in the household until 'rescued' and taken into the light by teams from the higher side of life. I have also, on many, many occasions, sat to read for people who are sitting in a circle that is completely wrong for them and felt myself sinking under the barrage of unseen vibrational baggage these people have picked up from that circle, either from other members of the circle or from unenlightened or unhappy spirits on the other side.

Circles should only be held with a reputable medium present to control them and to ensure that all members are safe and their chakras securely closed down at the end of each session and that no mischief is allowed entry to the proceedings.

If a circle works and its members gel and are sitting for the right reasons, it should very quickly become a closed circle (one to which no new members are admitted) so as to protect its integrity. If you ever sit in a circle and sense that something is wrong, don't feel embarrassed or that you're letting someone down by wanting to leave – listen to your inner self, head for the door and never look back! Never ignore or subdue your spiritual senses if they are telling you to get out of there – otherwise your guides will have great difficulty in protecting you and you will be in considerable danger.

In conclusion, not all the spirits you will encounter during your spiritual journey will be enlightened ones with pure motives. However, with discipline and common sense and a dedication to God and the right *motives* in all that you do spiritually, you can successfully steer clear of them and, with experience, eventually learn to recognise them and send them on their way.

Question: What, exactly, is the relationship between me as a spirit and my physical body?

A. Society on earth has long bought into the deception that you *are* your physical body and your physical mind. When you become ill, for example, it is usually the physical body *only* which is treated, when in actuality attempting to heal this single aspect of the whole person in many cases does nothing more than place a temporary bandage on the outward – physical – manifestations of a core problem that has as its roots a distress or imbalance in the *spirit*. One day, when we understand our true, holistic nature as be-ings, we will learn to treat the body, mind and *spirit* of a dis-eased person in order to bring about complete and permanent cures for all types of illness.

In reality you and your physical body exist as two linked yet *separate* consciousnesses. Your physical body has been created specifically to anchor your spirit self to this physical level during your stay on earth and to allow you movement and expression within the atmospheric conditions of this world. It is composed not only of the heavier atoms of the earth plane from which its physical manifestation is constructed, but also of finer, etheric matter – subtle spirit energies that permeate and animate that denser material. The vibrations of your physical body, when the energies continuously radiating outwards from God consciousness through your soul to that body are flowing as they should, are in synchronisation with the vibratory rate of the real you and the two of you co-exist in a harmonious but temporary symbiosis* (under the normal, God-intended flow of these energies you should enjoy a state of balanced mental and physical health). You need your physical body in order to exist and to function and to interact in this world and your physical body needs you as the energetic house-guest that steers it through life and maintains its form and function.

Your physical body, however, also possesses an intelligence *of its own,* enabling it to operate both in harmony with your spirit self and, at the same time, autonomously. *Conscious* thought and will are not required on your part to keep your body functioning. It needs the connection with you in order to obtain its energies, but whilst that connection exists the body is perfectly capable of carrying out its myriad functions without you having to apply any conscious effort to the business of keeping it 'alive'. Do you constantly have to will your heart to beat? Or your blood to flow? Or your lungs to take in oxygen? Or your stomach to digest food? The body knows what it has to do and, as long as it is looked after by you and fed subconsciously by you with a continuous flow of light-energy, it will continue to do its job until the time comes for it to cease functioning on your behalf. The physical body can only become sick when the energies from the God source, flowing to and through your soul, then outwards into the body, become blocked before they can enter and energise that body, and this only happens when the soul temporarily falls out of harmony with God thinking, its own thoughts and beliefs causing the blockage.

The physical body is your point of connection to this physical world, a reference point that enables you to look in a mirror and say *this is me*, then to look around and make the distinction of *this is not me*, physically speaking, with regards to the rest of physicality. It is the kingdom and boundaries of the physical you. It sets you, as a perceiving physical being, apart from other physical matter and completes the illusion of separatness (you are, in fact, a part of everything) that is necessary for the growth of your soul. It is a vehicle and a home for your spirit and also the recognition point by which other incarnated souls define what is you and what is not you; where you end and they begin.

Your thoughts and expectations and beliefs affect and adjust and sculpt your physical body. Unknowingly, you feed it daily with so much more than food, second by second pouring into it, via the physical mind, a complex mix of instructions based, to a great extent, on illusion and false expectations. Continually, via both your subconscious and conscious minds, you instruct the body to exist in a specific state. To be well. Or to be ill. Or to be fat. Or to be thin. Or to be tired. Or to be energetic. Or to be old. You command it to conform to your conceptions of how it should be and it acts on and complies with the instructions you channel into it, via the output of your physical mind, microsecond by microsecond. Let's take one single belief as an example – that of advancing age. At any stage in your life you expect to look in a mirror and see a face and figure before you which ties in with a certain set of characteristics representative of the age group to which you currently belong – that is, you and society expect your body to look and to act in a certain way dependent on how long it has been on earth. You therefore unwittingly programme your physical mind daily with your own expectations, based on the ingrained beliefs of society, of how you feel – *believe* – you should appear and act. Your body, obeying the instructions you give to it, follows your commands (your beliefs and expectations) and reconstructs its physiognomy accordingly. It responds to your every wish and builds you an exact representation of what you expect to see in the mirror. Were you, using the creative power of thought, to programme it in a different way – for example believing, *really believing*, in a healthier, more youthful you, then those aspects of the physical are what the body would work to manifest around you.

The spirit you is connected to your physical body by a silver umbilical cord. This conduit feeds your body with the energies it needs to maintain its form and function and to be bound specifically to you, even when you, the spirit, are not actually residing within it. As souls most of us step outside of and travel away from our bodies during the night, when only the physical aspects of our being need rest and regeneration. The soul, freed from the constraints of physical consciousness and fatigue, can then travel to other areas of the world if it so wishes, or to the spirit realms for rest, tuition, companionship, healing, or to continue whatever work the soul is involved in in its greater life. The silver cord allows the travelling soul to maintain a connection with its physical body and to continue to donate energy to it whilst it is away from its physical home. The cord can stretch over enormous distances without severing, so no matter how far the soul moves away from its physical body whilst astral travelling, the physical body is still in contact with and connected to its owner. At the point of death (an event, by the way, which is programmed into the physical body and its surrounding energies – but that is a subject for discussion in another volume) the silver cord severs and the physical body ceases to function. The consciousness of the body is withdrawn and returns to the pool of life consciousness from which it came, the physical aspect of the body returns to the earth from which *it* came (where its atoms, as it breaks down, are cleansed and neutralised vibrationally by the earth so that they can become another physical expression of life without holding onto the vibrations of their last host) and the soul returns to the spirit realms from which *it* came.

As an example of how body and soul are two linked yet separate entities, each able to function independently whilst the connection between them exists, let me conclude this section by telling you a little story. A few years ago the boyfriend of one of my hairdresser's assistants was involved in an accident and, as a result of this, fell into a coma. Whilst sitting in the chair having my hair cut one day I suddenly became clairvoyantly aware of a young man who wished to speak to the girl. He told me the type of music he liked, mentioned a month that was in some way significant and said he had spoken with his grandfather on the spirit side and had been informed by him that it wasn't yet time for him to pass over. I gave this information to the girl who, a little shocked, cited the month as the one in which she and her boyfriend had met and confirmed the type of music he liked. He then informed me that she held his hand in a specific way when she went to see him in the hospital and also adjusted the light above his bed. Again, she confirmed that this was the case. I reassured her that it was unlikely the young man was going to die as he'd told me his grandfather had informed him it wasn't his time to do so. Sure enough, the young man eventually came out of his coma and returned to this world... where his physical body, which had been operating quite independently of him for some time (obviously still being donated essential life energies via the young man's silver chord) was ready for him to take up residence again.

This is one of the reasons why a body that has been given organs from another body usually has to be drugged into submission so that it does not reject the new tissue. The host body

108

senses the differing vibrations between itself and the introduced organs and refuses initially to incorporate them into its system. In many cases, over time, the host body gradually impresses the new organs with its dominant vibrational signature and the urge to reject them diminishes.

Question: What is the difference between a medium and a psychic? Are we all psychic? Are we all mediumistic?

A. I have to chuckle these days when I see my fellow mediums often being promoted in the press or on television under the banner of 'psychic mediums'. Having worked as a copywriter for many years (until God required me to change horses completely in mid-stream in order to to work for *Him*) I can fully understand that the writers behind the publicity are trying to cover every possible base in an attempt to draw attention to their clients. So why the chuckle? Because *every* medium you will ever meet is psychic – *and so are you*. We are *all* psychic. We are *all* spirits and, whether we acknowledge it or not, whether we believe in it or not, we are all able, at a sub-conscious level, to pick up the moods and feelings and sudden anxieties of people we have a family or friendship connection with at a distance. We are all parts of the same thing – of God – and, as God's children, as parts of the same spiritual body of consciousness, we are all connected to each other, which is why, at times, we can sense another's pain, or joy, or frustration, or urgent need to contact us, without us needing to be in direct physical contact with them.

Allow me to demonstrate your own psychic abilities to you. How often have you thought of a friend or a relative and, a moment later, the telephone has rung only for you to

110

discover that the person you've just been thinking about is on the other end of the line? How often have you then joked with that person, saying, "Well, that's a coincidence. I was just this minute thinking about you. I must be psychic!" There's many a true word spoken in jest. In such instances, what actually happens is this: In order to ring you the person who wants to make contact with you first has to *think* about you. In considering ringing you they instantly bring images of you, and of their connections to you, into their mind. By thinking strongly of you they form a conscious energy link with you at that moment as a soul and their will – their desire to contact you – automatically extends a chord of energy from their spirit self to your spirit self. In other words, they make a spiritual connection – a spiritual call – to you *before* they ever pick up the telephone to contact you by physical means. The minute they make that connection your psychic 'receiving centre' picks up the link with them telepathically – *psychically* – at a sub-conscious level and your physical mind begins to produce thoughts and images of them. The telephone rings and you have no need to guess who is on the other end of it – you already know because *you are psychic*. Consider how many times in your life you have also known, without being told, that a member of your family or a close friend is in trouble; or how many times you have known ahead of schedule what, precisely, is going to happen to you in certain situations before it actually does so on a physical level and you have to admit that the evidence for you, personally, being psychic, is hard to refute.

In many magazines covering the paranormal or spiritual matters you will see, running alongside advertisements for mediums (and *psychic* mediums, haha!) advertisements for *psychics*, with 'psychic hot lines' (services offered by a psychic over the telephone) being a current favourite. Psychics do not advertise themselves as mediums and are, in effect, providing quite a different service from that offered by a medium. So, what *is* the difference between a psychic and a medium? Let me first say that in the following explanation I am expressing no bias towards one form of service or another – I am simply pointing out how these two exacting areas of spiritual work can and should be distinguished from each other.

Psychics have the ability to tune into and 'read' the normally hidden energy signals that we all carry around with us and that offer information to those of sufficient psychic sensitivity regarding aspects of our current state of be-ing. Our past, present and, to some extent, future 'histories' can be read by attuning to the psychic energies we constantly radiate as spiritual beings. A psychic tunes in to those energies by connecting psychically with the person they are conducting a reading for. At a psychic level relevant data regarding the person – mental tendencies, state of health, emotional situations – can all can be discerned and interpreted by a gifted psychic. These energies can be likened to a constantly updating identity card that provides the psychic with information concerning the sitter's life.

Some psychics use tarot cards to exactly the same ends. The person desiring a reading is first asked to handle the cards and, in doing so, subconsciously influences – *impregnates temporarily* – the cards with their own psychic energies. The cards, when spread out by the psychic in specific patterns, then express many aspects of what is happening and what is shortly to happen (as we understand the concept of time) around the sitter by presenting themselves to the psychic in a sequence that has been predetermined by the sitter having handling them.

Mediums should, if they are working correctly, be tuning in not to the sitter, but to the still, small voice of the spirit world talking to them on the sitter's behalf. When sitting with someone a medium shifts part of his or her consciousness from this world to another area of being – another level of reality. It is rather like tuning into a different station on your television set. If you're watching one station (i.e. this level of consciousness) you will not receive images and information from any other stations (the spirit worlds) until you make a conscious decision to change frequency. Having opened up to a higher vibration of consciousness the medium is then totally reliant on his or her guides working behind the scenes to build around the medium the energies necessary for successful communication and then to bring through family and friendship links to the person the medium is sitting with via their instrument. The medium cannot function without these people talking to him or her and passing on information and advice which the medium then relays to the sitter. At the end of the reading the medium is told it is time to 'shut down' by one of his or her guides and their consciousness is brought back to this world – to a renewed immersion in and compatibility with this particular vibration of being – so that the medium is no longer picking up speech, images, personalities and sensations from higher levels of consciousness. The medium must also aid the shut-down process by consciously closing their spiritual energy centres – the chakras – so that they are once again receiving information from this level of consciousness only.

On an number of occasions people have come up to me in a church following a service and, with reference to mediumship and the demonstration that has just taken place, said something along the lines of, "But we can all do this, can't we? It's just a matter of practice, isn't it?" The implication being, of course, that we are all psychic (which we are) and that we are all mediumistic (which we are *not*). People who are mediumistic are 'put together' in a slightly different way than people who are not. The various states of being that comprise a human being are usually nested and locked very tightly together in order that the person might function as they are supposed to whilst within this physical sphere of consciousness. Not so with mediums. The bonds between the various vehicles – bodies – that house the medium's spirit are more loosely and flexibly connected than is the norm, allowing the medium, with practice, to in effect will their consciousness to take a side-step out of their bodies to meet the incoming stream of spiritual information half way. Then, once spirit communication has taken place, the medium is able to pull the focal point of his or her consciousness back into their physical bodies and operate fairly normally (!) on this level of perception. I say *fairly* normally because our tendency to live partially in two worlds at the same time – and to not quite live totally in this world – often makes us seem eccentric to the rest of the population. Hardly surprising when you consider that we spend a great deal of our existence on earth quite literally *out of our minds*.

If you are mediumistic – if you have been chosen to serve God in this way at some stage during your life, then it *will* happen, and you will have already been given indications that you have a gift in this area. If, in addition to the psychic occurrences common to us all, some of which I described earlier in this section, you have also at times sensed or seen people from the spirit side of life, or experienced super-real dreams occasionally, or had sudden flashes of foresight, then (almost certainly) you are an embryonic medium. If you wish to nurture these tendencies (you have a choice, as with every aspect of your life, but you will find that the gift tends to pull you back onto a path that leads to you developing and using it if at first you decide to turn away from it) and refine them to the point where you can be of service to God and to the spirit worlds, then all it takes on your part is a willingness to do the work and heaven and earth will be moved to ensure that you receive the guidance and the teaching you will need to understand and expand your gifts. You needn't worry about where this guidance and teaching will come from – if you wish to work for God and have the gift, the means of expressing that gift will manifest around you on your life path. All you have to do is say, "Yes, Father, I am willing to do your work," and the people and situations you will need in order to develop your gift will be drawn to you – and you to them – like a magnet. Your sincere desire to work for the light *and only the light* (i.e. not to use the gift as a means of drawing attention to yourself) is all it takes – simply **Be Still** and God will do the rest.

Finally, if you are considering investing in a reading, which option should you take? Should you visit a psychic or a medium? *It's your choice.* First listen to the promptings of your inner voice. If you cannot decide, having separate readings with both a reputable psychic and a reputable medium will enable you to decide which service is more appropriate to what you are looking for in life. Generally speaking, if you simply wish to know more of your future, arrange to see a psychic. If you wish to contact the spirit world, to receive information from your friends and relatives who have passed over and to perhaps be put in touch with your guides and given advice regarding any spiritual gifts you may have and where they might take you, contact a medium.

A final word of caution, however. Some people go from medium to medium, psychic to psychic, sitting for reading after reading and becoming, in effect, *psychic junkies*, expecting every aspect of their lives to be sorted by higher authority for them in advance. We are here to give you a boost and an insight and help at certain times in your lives, not to live your lives for you. Consult us, yes, but do not expect a medium or a psychic to be able to plot out your whole life for you so that you don't have to lift a finger or ever again have to decide for yourself what to do in challenging circumstances. Your lives are yours to make of what you wish – and living them daily to the full, and tackling the challenges they will bring to you – *your way* – is what you are here on earth to do.

Question. Will we be judged for our past actions on earth when we pass to the higher side of life?

A. The traditional view of heaven and hell as destinations God will dispatch you to dependent on how you have lived your life whilst on this planet are quite wrong. God does not and will *never, ever judge you*. Nor will the highly evolved guides and the angels who have been assigned to you during your earthly life. It is not their place to do so and, as spiritually enlightened beings, they would never seek to do so. You are a part of God and he loves you *unconditionally*, whatever you may have thought during your life on earth and whatever you may have done – or failed to do – with your time here. How could a loving God condemn you to an eternity of suffering? Could you condemn one of your own fingers or toes, then plunge them into an eternity of pain? The traditional vision of an everlasting hell where one is tortured forever without hope of peace or redemption, one that many, many souls on earth still subscribe to, is in reality a fictional place formulated by religion as a means of controlling its followers.

Having said that, there *is,* however, a severe judge you will one day inevitably meet and who will examine your entire life on earth in minute detail, weighing whether, in his or her judgement, it has been a success or a failure (or some combination of the two concepts) with regard to the evolution it was intended to bring to your soul.

Picture the scene. You have recently passed over and have arrived in one of the spirit realms. It is a beautiful world of light. The landscape, your companions, the sights, sounds, scents and feelings of this place are quite exquisite. It is such a relief to have left behind the worries and the challenges and the aches and pains of your former life on earth. No one here forces you to do anything you do not wish to do. No-one criticises you. No-one bothers you. There is companionship when you desire it and perfect peace and solitude when you don't. Things are wonderful for a while and you truly feel you are in heaven. As the days pass, however, you sense an increasing unease from within which you finally pinpoint as a need expressed from your spirit to somehow draw a line under your earthly affairs. This feeling troubles you, as up to this point you had thought that physical death had done a pretty good job of drawing a line under your earthly affairs for you!

One day a knock comes to the door of the beautiful house you are living in.

You open it to find an angel – a being of light – standing on your doorstep.

He/she smiles and says, "It is time," and you feel a knot suddenly form in your stomach.

The angel leads you through perfect streets and leafy avenues to a little movie theatre.

You both go in through the double doors and find that there is no-one else in the building.

You walk through the empty foyer and enter the screening area. As you sit down in one of the plush seats the angel explains that you are about to be treated to a free film show and that he/she will be just outside should you need him/her.

The lights go down, the curtains pull back and there, on the silver screen, begins an epic you had never expected to see. The film's title is *This is my Life*, and you watch in morbid fascination as, from birth to grave, every single aspect of the life you have just lived on earth unfolds again before you.

You relive, with a warm feeling inside, the good you have done.

You also cringe and shrink down in your seat as you realise how badly you have treated people at times and how much pain you have caused them. For a split second you somehow actually *become* each of the people you have hurt, experiencing their emotions first hand and feeling exactly as they felt whilst they were on the receiving end of your words and deeds, your actions and inactions.

Every thought, every comment, every action, every single thing you ever did during your past life is there on the screen. It is as though you had been carrying some type of unseen recording device with you on your journey through life from the moment you were born to the moment you passed over.

The film ends and you find you are shaking and that tears are rolling down your cheeks. How could you have *said* those things? How could you have *done* those things? How could you have *failed to do* so many things? Your transgressions against others – and against yourself – are now so obvious. You feel ashamed and humbled.

The angel reenters the cinema and sits next to you, radiating love towards you.

"Now, now," he/she says. "You really mustn't be so hard on yourself. You did, after all, get a great many things right but there are also areas where you need to polish up your act a bit if you want to progress further into infinity."

"I'll take you back to your home now. Then, after you've had a good, long rest and some time to think I'll call on you again and we can both sit down with your team of advisers. They will then suggest ways in which you might further refine and uplift the vibrational quality of your soul. Perhaps they will recommend that going back down to earth to work a few things out in another life would be a good idea. Perhaps they will propose quite a different existence in a completely different area of reality. Perhaps they will formulate other ways in which you can progress by carrying out some specialised and selfless work right here in the spiritual realms."

"Nothing they will suggest to you will be a command. You have the right to refuse any plan they put forward. You have free will and nothing will happen to you if you don't agree with their proposals. You can stay on this plane in your present circumstances indefinitely. However, should you eventually feel the need to leave your present surroundings and to move forwards – and I have to tell you that that day will come – you *will* need to work on the areas where your actions and inactions prevented your soul from progressing so that you can successfully increase your vibrational rate and gain access to the higher spheres of existence beyond this one."

You thank the angel, close the door, sit down in your comfortable armchair and, with a shudder, realise your recent life on earth has just been reviewed by the harshest, most unforgiving judge you could have ever had the misfortune to sit before ... *yourself*.

Question: What is the purpose of spirit communication and mediumship?

A. When I ask this question of an audience at a 'question and answer' session in a church or hall hands shoot up and a great many people eagerly tell me that the purpose of spirit communication is to prove the existence of life after death. I then have to tactfully inform them that this is not actually the case.

True, spirit communication with regard to providing links to departed family members offers comfort to the bereaved and evidence of an existence beyond this one, but there is a far more important purpose behind the phenomena.

Bearing in mind that spirit communication requires a great deal of energy and effort, both from the medium and from his or her team of workers on the higher side of life, ask yourself why all this energy is being expended just to prove that there is a life after death. Logically, *why bother* taking such pains and going to such great lengths in order to convince people of an existence that is there and waiting for every soul when they leave this world, regardless of whether they believe in it or not? *What is the point* when there are far more interesting things to do in the spirit realms than to wade back through the heavy matter of this level of consciousness in order to tell someone on earth that their grandad is fine and likes the new hat they bought last Wednesday?

The true purpose of spirit communication is the transmission of a universal message that permeates the individual messages given – an unspoken implication hidden in plain sight within every clairvoyant message that has ever been given and will ever be given at any time, at any location around our world. It is, quite simply, this: *Brother. Sister. You are not going to die...* **How, then, are you going to live?**

If you are not going to die, *and you are not*, and if everything that you do is not secret and private to you at all but is known about and recorded in the very fabric of your existence, *and it is*, then there is no escaping the consequences of every single action you take and every single thought you think whilst you are here. Those consequences, those ripples that you cause in the great ocean of be-ing, will either help you to evolve as a soul or *they will hinder your spiritual progress beyond a certain point until you work them out through your future actions*.

In other words, every day of your life is a vitally important day, because every thought you think and every action you take during that day has an effect on your spiritual future. There is no escaping it – you are building your spiritual tomorrow, and the *kind* of spiritual tomorrow you will experience, through the way you are living your life today. Shouldn't we, therefore, considering the aforementioned fact and also considering that we do not know the date upon which we are scheduled to return to the spirit worlds, live each day of our lives very carefully indeed and as spiritually as we are able to, and treat others on earth as we would were this to indeed be our last day here?

It cannot be argued that we have got something very wrong in society. If we had got things very *right* the world would be a far different place than the chaotic and violent manifestation that is currently around us. War and crime and cruelty would cease to exist. We would be tolerant, caring, loving people with concern and support for others and respect for ourselves and our planet. Spirit communication, once you dig beneath the individual messages of comfort and support, offers a new blueprint for life, an understanding of the laws of the universe and how to recognise them, use them and live harmoniously within them; a different way of living – of *being* – that *actually works* for us all because it is God's way. Waiting in the wings to speak through your mediums to those who would listen are countless evolved souls who passionately wish to reveal to us great insights and truths, enabling us to finally heal this world, each other and ourselves.

We have to be careful, therefore, not to fall into the 'clairvoyance trap' as we seek out spirit communication. Alongside those wonderfully spiritual people I regularly meet in spiritualist churches there are usually those at any meeting who do not care for any form of address that might actually teach them something, and indeed are not concerned for anyone else's suffering or problems. They look at their watches during prayers and teachings. They fidget. They simply cannot wait to get to the 'clairvoyant bit', because all they want is a message – *any message* as long as the medium comes to them. They pull at and divert the vibrations that are coming from the higher side of life and can sometimes take a medium away from the person the communication is actually intended for. Such souls have fallen into the clairvoyance trap. Mediumship has become, for them, an entertainment. Something to amuse them in spiritualist churches or in public halls or even in public houses and social clubs (and it makes me cringe to think that this is actually taking place these days, because the spirit world and your own departed family and friends should be approached with respect and with love, not with a cigarette in one hand and a pint in the other!).

No. No. *NO!* Let us please be enlightened enough to recognise that clairvoyance is trying to bring us its universal message and to therefore create venues and atmospheres within which high teachers from the spirit world can revisit this earth through our mediums to enlighten us. For the true desire of our spirit communicators is to bring light into the world; to illuminate the dark corners within the minds of men and women. To bring through the light of understanding which changes and which heals, light which shines on the true path and the true way, light which *sets us free*. Let us *demand* this quality of communication from our mediums, and in discipline and with dedication let us sit with them week upon week and year upon year and let us

build spiritual power and love around them so that they ca
bring forth *spiritual truth*. Let us understand that they need
us and our help so that they can continue to work on our
behalf. Let us seek out the highest and the best always in our
spirit communicators, because the true purpose of spirit
communication is to bring out the very best in us all, to
show us what we are truly capable of as spirits on earth and
to change this level of consciousness for the better,
completely and forever.

Ladies and gentlemen, that has to be worth working
towards!